LESSONS
LEARNT

THE STORY OF YOUNG MAI

ALFREDA WILLIAMS

ISBN 978-1-64468-497-9 (Paperback)
ISBN 978-1-64468-498-6 (Digital)

Covenant Books, Inc.
11661 Hwy 707
Murrells Inlet, SC 29576
www.covenantbooks.com

INTRODUCTION

For over twenty-five years, she had tried to write HerStory. She had plenty of aspiration, but hardly any inspiration. She would start and stop. Start and stop. The story of her life. Trying so hard to start but then to stop. Always *the Procrastinator. Why, oh why, do I procrastinate so much?* Nevertheless, she kept on going back to Her Story. Intermittently, a little bit here, a little bit there. By serendipity, she met a man who, though himself barely able to read, told her to write a book. That she must write a book. And he was not the first one to tell her so. So, she knew it was something she *had* to do. She didn't know why. But she had to. She *had* a story to tell. She just had to tell her story.

She was a prolific reader and would inundate herself with a copious number of religious, motivational, and self-help books. She would buy numerous books, putting them aside to read when she needed fortification against and to free her mind from the stresses and worries that she found herself constantly battling. Often, she would resort to these books when she was depressed, bouncing off the walls and ceilings, reeling from stress and under attack from her constant companion, that good ole devil. Sometimes she just couldn't shake him loose. He often manifested himself through her family, friends, and jobs. He was always there, attacking her, trying to make her fail, questioning her value, her self-esteem, and her reason for living. She was in a constant battle with him, trying to believe that she did have value and that she was okay. Inwardly though, she felt that she wasn't really good enough to live her life as she pleased because her family and colleagues made so many demands of her. She felt that she was expected to always give of herself to others. "To whom much is given, much is required," her pastor would quote from the Bible.

Consequently, she was always putting others' needs above her own, doing good for them, sacrificing herself, and becoming too exhausted from meeting others' needs to meet her own.

Although she had made some good career moves, her personal and emotional lives were tormented. While maintaining a happy façade in the presence of family and friends, inside she was really hurting. During the last few years of her life, she had chosen to withdraw from most social activities rather than deal with the pain and uncertainty of roller-coaster emotional experiences. She realized that she had been suffering from an insidious form of depression that often inhibited her from enjoying and taking the reins of her life. To avoid facing up to the malaise that impeded her from constructive functioning, she had chosen to bury herself in various jobs and mundane church activities. She avoided relationships with men, numbing her feelings by adopting a laissez-faire attitude, having been disappointed by so many failed past relationships. When she chose to engage in amorous relationships, it was always with the attitude that it would not last, that she was just passing through, although, from time to time, she would fall in love, only to have her heart broken again. And, to be perfectly honest, she made poor decisions about whom to fall in love with.

Then, one day after years of procrastination, stress, and anxiety, she read and internalized a motivational saying that gave her the inspiration to complete her book or at least take a good stab at it. "When all is said and done, it's really up to you." She had heard that saying so many times without seriously thinking about it. But, on that particular day, for some reason, it hit her like a heavy hammer inside her brains. She was forced to do some serious introspection. *Damn, it is up to me,* she thought. *Why,* she asked, *why have I always put others' needs ahead of my own? Why,* she asked, *why haven't I ordered my personal life as I have my professional life?*

All my life, I have been letting life happen to me. And I've been blaming life, chance, luck, and fate, whatever. Always being a victim. I'm tired being a victim. Now it's time for me to take hold of my life, to do something that I, not someone else, feel is important. For too long, I've put others' needs ahead of my own.

For too long, I've been throwing my pearls to swine, letting others benefit from my time and talents. It's time for me to benefit. It's time for me to do something I've always wanted to do. It's time for me to finish my book.

Then, one day she read a speech, often attributed to Nelson Mandela, which said in part

> *Our deepest fear is not that we are inadequate.*
> *Our deepest fear is that we are powerful beyond*
> *measure. It is our light, not our darkness, that*
> *most frightens us. We ask ourselves, "Who am I*
> *to be brilliant, gorgeous, talented and fabulous?"*
> *Actually, who are you not to be? Your playing*
> *small does not serve the world. There is nothing*
> *enlightened about 'shrinking' so that other people*
> *won't feel insecure around you. We were born*
> *to make manifest the glory that is within us. It*
> *is not within 'some of us', it is within everyone!*
> *And as we let our light shine, we unconsciously*
> *give other people permission to do the same.*
> *As we are liberated from our own fears, our*
> *presence automatically liberates others.*

Wow! That's deep, she thought. Why have I always denigrated myself? Why have I thought I was not worthy? And when did I acquire this ingrained sense of inferiority? Why have I not stepped forward as I should have? Why have I been afraid to "shine?" She had to do some real soul-searching introspection to find the answers to those questions. And the only way she could really do that down-deep soul searching was to thoroughly examine her life, every phase of it. And the best way she knew to do this was to write about her life. HerStory.

And so, she took a deep, hard, long breath and asked for that *Special Inspiration*. That kind of inspiration that she had so often read about in the Bible and in the stories of great men and women. That Joan of Arc inspiration and determination. That walking around the walls of Jericho inspiration. That little engine that could determination. Although she had studied the writing styles of various authors in an attempt to write a "professional" book, she decided to abandon those styles and depend upon her *higher source* for direction. When she was ready to begin her book, she began by writing from her heart, through her heart, with the words and flow dictated by her heart. She decided to write about something with which she was most familiar—herself. Starting with the early years. Hoping to remember the later years. And hoping that her struggles would help enlighten someone else who was struggling with life's issues. To know that they are not alone, fighting the demons of fear, self-doubt, and inferiority. That, although it may seem like an insurmountable battle, it can be won. Sometimes, only after years and years and years of battling. Just keep in mind that all things are possible.

Lord, help me, she prayed. *Help me tell this story. Let it be an inspiration for someone. Let it uplift somebody's spirit, while releasing me from my own demons.*

THE EARLY YEARS

Playing in the red dirt in Natchez
Staying with my godparents
Going to church on Sundays
Traveling to Up North to Chicago with my sisters
Living with my mother, sisters, my aunt and her
    husband upon arriving to Chicago
Living in rat-infested tenements
Going to church several times a week and playing
    with my friends there
Wishing that the church's pastor was my father
Living in our first decent apartment; playing in
    the front yard with Berniece
Meeting my future stepfather
Moving back Down South to Natchez to live
    with my grandparents
Visiting my godparents
Playing with my cousins Down South
Attending elementary school Down South
Returning to Chicago with my grandmother
    after one year Down South
Learning that my mother was living with my future
    stepfather and that I had a new brother
My disappointment in not being able to return
    to Natchez with my grandmother
My mother's marriage to my stepfather
Refusing to repeat fifth grade because I had
    attended school Down South
Playing with my school and neighborhood friends

Garfield Center Field House
Being molested by my stepfather
Visiting with my cousins in Wisconsin
Graduating from eighth grade

I tried too hard. I had always tried too hard. During my child-hood, I was the Class Buffoon. The Clown. The Tomboy. Trying to please others. Trying so hard to get others to like me. Covering up my self-perceived faults and defects by my over-the-years carefully developed system of histrionics.

I intensely detested being born a girl. I never wanted to be a girl. My greatest sorrow during childhood was that I was born a girl. Not that I was a lesbian, had lesbian tendencies, or thoughts or any-thing like that. But I felt that being born a girl was so unfair. Back then, when I was growing up, things were so much different for girls. No equality of the sexes. Boys got to do *everything!* Climb trees and fences, fight, make war, and sleep with *everybody* (in a very literal sense) and yet maintain a respected, if not admirable reputation, especially the more bodies they slept with.

But *girls!* That was another story. Girls couldn't do this and couldn't do that. Girls couldn't be just girls. No, we had to be the future mothers of tomorrow. We couldn't play on the school's baseball team, basketball team, football team, or in any game considered to be a "boys" game. Girls couldn't pick up heavy packages, climb trees or fences, or do anything that might jeopardize our precious future ability to bear children. So I had to learn how to prepare for motherhood while the boys learned how to play and make war with one another. I had to learn how to clean house, cook, sew, do the laundry, and take care of my younger siblings. From my perspective, life was just downright unfair because I wanted to be "one of the boys." And it just could not be so. I had a problem with this sexual inequality stuff. It was painful. Not being able to do what you wanted to do because of societal norms. I was like a pimple waiting to burst, which accounts for many of the problems I had when I was growing up. *Lesson learnt—no matter how much you want it to be so, sometimes life just isn't fair.*

***

Born in Natchez, I can't remember too much about my early childhood years, when I was a very little girl in the South. I can't remember too much of my life before my fifth birthday. I do remember being in the South, playing in the fields and eating the red Mississippi clay dirt that seemed to ooze like goo through my fingers and on my tongue. It was so delicious. So mouthwatering and soothing to my mouth, dissolving down my throat like soft custard. I can barely remember my mother Cora, my two sisters, my grandparents, and other relatives. But I fondly remember my godparents. I scarcely remember one other sister, Delores, who, at the age of four years old, was killed by a motorcycle. I can't remember my father. Years later, I learned that I couldn't remember him because he wasn't there. Forty-nine years later, in a conversation with Mama and sister Edna, I learned that I couldn't remember Delores because Edna reminded Mama that Delores died before I was born. But for forty-some years, Mama planted the memory of Delores in my mind (*you remember playing with her, don't you? Remember when…?*), so much so that I actually believed that I remembered playing with her. *Lesson learnt— trust your own memories.*

***

I did have some vague, early childhood memories of my grandparents. I tried to avoid Grandpa Malone because he seemed so formidable and mean. So tall, so black, with a perpetual scowl on his face. Grandma Hattie had a sweet spirit which I, even in my youthful innocence, sensed.

On the other hand, I had glowing memories of my godparents Miss Mary and Mr. Wilmer. I would often spend weekends and even weeks-on-end with them. They were kind, loving, and protective. With them, I was truly pampered. They had an oversized backyard with brilliant, multicolored flowers and lots of flourishing vegetables—tomatoes, collard greens, beans, cabbage, and green peppers. They also had a few chickens, a scrawny rooster, a couple of fat pigs, and two playful dogs. Although initially timid when I first encountered the dogs, in time I became enamored with them. We would romp around that big backyard together all day long. I could play in the backyard's sandy dirt for hours on end without being scolded. Clean or dirty, my godparents equally loved me. And I loved them so much, so very, very much, much more than my mother and grandparents. I had a special god-brother, Richard, who treated me just like his own little sister. No distinction. Just love everywhere.

Being at my godparents' house was like being in another world, even though it was within a five-block walking distance of my mother's house. And my godparents had an indoor toilet! At Mama's house, we had an outdoor toilet, called an outhouse, which the older children and adults used. An outhouse was a shed with a seat perched upon a deep hole that was dug into to the ground for purposes of urinating and defecating. It reeked to high heaven because there was no mechanism to flush the waste. Instead, when the hole in the outhouse was filled with waste, it was covered up with dirt and a new outhouse was built. The smaller kids used a tin bucket to eliminate their bodily fluids and waste. Every morning, Mama would empty the tin waste bucket into that foul, smelly outhouse. At my godparents' house, I only had to hoist my tiny body onto the toilet stool, eliminate my waste, and flush the toilet. No foulness there.

My godparents' living room was truly a thing of beauty to behold. So warm, so friendly, so "make-yourself-at-home-ish." It was decorated with diverse dolls of many colors and nationalities, some made of porcelain, some of china and some of cloth.

Oversized china lamps were arranged on the coffee and end tables which were covered with dainty, spotless white doilies crocheted by my godmother. The shadow box was filled with multiple figurines, some religious, mostly antiques. There was a gigantic piano in the middle of the living room that Miss Mary would often play for me, teaching me many Christian songs like *Yes, Jesus Loves Me, This Little Light of Mine* and *He's Got the Whole World in His Hands.*

Best of all, I had my own bed and my own bedroom. I didn't have to share my privacy with anyone, unlike at my mother's house where I had to share the bedroom with my two sisters. At my godparents' house, bedtime was a joy rather than a punishment. My bed was a big poster bed with huge, rounded posts on all four corners.

It was a high bed; I had to use a step stool to put my teeny weenie body in it. It was always covered with a pretty quilt, handmade by Miss Mary, and sundry fluffy pillows. I would hoist my tiny body onto that big bed and dream sweet, wonderful dreams. Dreams of ever-loving love for my godparents. Always happy dreams. Life-will-always-be-so-wonderful dreams.

Godfather Wilmer was a deliveryman for one of the local milk and juice companies. He was a tall, extremely handsome, jolly, copper-toned man with a deep voice who would often set me on his lap and tell fairy tales, teach me Bible lessons, and sing songs to me. He would always bring home fresh-squeezed orange juice in pretty quart-sized glass bottles, which was a delicacy for me because my family never had fresh-squeezed orange juice. I can still taste and smell the orange juice to this very day. So cold, so tingly, so good, so fresh, so sweet.

Godmother Mary did not work, and so she was free to lovingly attend to my every whim all day long. I did not have to share her with anyone, unlike my mother who had to split her free time with my two other sisters. Richard, Miss Mary's son, was much older than I and did not require much of Miss Mary's attention. Miss Mary was a short woman, with long, pretty straight hair, somewhat bright-skinned, with a shrill voice. She liked to laugh and have a good time. She thoroughly enjoyed my company. Even later in my adult life, I can still hear Miss Mary's shrill voice, calling out to me like it was yesterday. "Maaiii, Maaiii! Chile, come in here and eat your lunch!"

And Miss Mary could cook! They had food that my mother never had. Most mornings they would have bacon or sausage for breakfast, something that we never had at my mother's house. All my mother could afford was salt pork. Miss Mary would cook expensive cuts of meat and fancy vegetables like broccoli and cauliflower, not the collard greens and cabbage that I often ate at home. And she always served me my favorite foods like fried chicken, smothered pork chops, oven-baked pork brisket, baked lamb chops and baked ham. Dinner was always followed with a dessert like luscious pound cake, delightful lemon pie, and tantalizing strawberry shortcake. Every dinner was like eating at the king's table. Godfather Wilmer would always say grace before we ate, and during dinner they would talk about their day. Godfather Wilmer would talk about his deliveries and people on his route that were sick or on vacation. Godmother Mary would talk about the church people and things that were happening in the neighborhood. And I would just listen, enthralled by their conversation, sometimes telling them about my exploits in the backyard with the dogs, chickens, birds, and pigs.

I had so much fun at my godparents and became so attached to them that Mama became quite alarmed that she was losing my affection. One day, after I had been at my godparents' house for about a week, out of the clear blue sky, she angrily marched to their house demanding that I return home, saying *"Give me my baby back."* With those words, she snatched me up and took me home. My visits to my godparents became shorter and less frequent. But I still loved them harder than any child could love anyone. I looked forward to seeing them in church every Sunday and cherished and relished being with them whenever I could. *Lesson learnt—yes, there truly is such a thing as unconditional love.*

***

When I was about four years old, Mama left to go Up North to Chicago for a better life, leaving care of her children to Grandpa Malone and Grandma Hattie. Months later, after she found a job and housing with a younger sister, she sent for me and my two sisters, Edna and Berniece. You should have seen us! Three little girls, ages twelve, five, and two, riding that great big Greyhound Bus all by ourselves, going Up North to be with our mother. So grown-up. My older sister Edna was in charge of us. And she did a doggone good job of caring for us during the trip, for she had learned her girlhood "preparation for motherhood" lessons well. Grandma Hattie packed us a "shoebox" lunch, consisting of fried chicken, bread, fruit, and pound cake—all packed in a shoebox.

During the long bus ride to Chicago, there were some things that happened that I didn't really quite understand. Like when the bus stopped at a restaurant for the passengers to eat. When we went into the restaurant to order some food, we were told to go to the rear, outside the restaurant, and order our food from the back counter— the "colored" counter. I didn't understand it because the counter was white, not colored. We couldn't sit down in the restaurant with the other patrons. But I didn't care. I was tired of eating the fried chicken sandwiches that Grandma Hattie had prepared for our trip. I was thrilled that we had enough money to order from the restaurant menu, even though we had to take it back to the bus to eat, where we sat in the back rows with the other Black passengers. And along the way on our ride Up North, I saw the special restrooms and water fountains just for me and my sisters and other Black people! They said Colored Only. *Wow,* I thought, *we have our own washrooms, although I don't know why we can't all use the same washroom.* It was years later that I learned about Jim Crow and that Grandma Hattie had packed the shoebox lunch because she knew that we would not be allowed into restaurants in the South. Years later, I also learned that "For Colored Only" washrooms were not special, that they were demeaning and racist, serving to separate Black folks from White folks and to reinforce the notion of white superiority. *Lesson learnt— although I didn't know its name, racism exists, whether you recognize it or not.* It was a lesson that repeated itself many times in my life.

***

Upon our arrival Up North, we happily joined Mama, who lived in a family building, with three floors of relatives, owned by one of my many cousins, all from Down South who had migrated Up North in search of a better life.

We lived in the garden apartment with our aunt Mamie, and her husband. Aunt Mamie always had lots of company in her house. Her apartment seemed to serve as a gateway for kinfolks who relocated to the North. Another aunt, Lillie, who had left the South, stayed with us briefly. She was real pretty with long straight hair, flawless chocolate brown skin, a curvaceous body, and sparkling white pretty teeth. She had lots of friends, mostly male, who often visited her. I didn't know how all of those people fit into that two bedroom apartment.

There was Uncle Jimmy (Aunt Mamie's husband), Aunt Mamie, Aunt Lillie, Mama, and us three little girls. The smaller bedroom was for Mama and Aunt Lillie. The small foyer had been converted into a bedroom in which we three girls slept and Aunt Mamie and Uncle Jimmy slept in the one big bedroom.

Aunt Mamie seemed to be a kindly but extremely strict woman. In fact, I was somewhat scared of her. She was very domineering, often talking in a too-loud abrasive voice. Uncle Jimmy, though, was a real kind man who, in many ways, reminded me of my godfather. I was a curious child, who constantly asked lots of questions, which was one reason Uncle Jimmy liked me so much. He would often romp and play with me, playing hide and seek, taking a generally fatherly interest in me, and always sneaking candy and cookies to me.

Although I was skinny, he would often tell the family that I was going to grow up to be a fine fox with big legs. And I would blush whenever he said it, although I wasn't quite sure what a "fox" was, but I took it to be a good thing.

Aunt Mamie, Aunt Lillie and Mama would often throw parties on the weekends, "rent parties" they called them. News of the parties was spread by word of mouth, and everyone attending had to pay a twenty-five-cent "admission fee" which was used to help pay for the rent, hence called "rent parties." Each party was teeming with plenty of food and music. Most times, there were at least twenty people at the parties. Twenty people in that little garden apartment! But somehow, they all managed to find a spot. Some at the kitchen table playing cards, others in the living room sitting around talking, and some dancing. Oh, what fun they had! Men and women. They would play cards, dance, and drink. Of course, I didn't know what they were drinking. All I knew was that the more they drank, the merrier they became, laughing and joking with each other, often speaking in boisterous voices. My sisters and I were relegated to my mother's bedroom while the adults were having fun. The adults would play card games for money, some of which Aunt Mamie took for a "cut." The money she took from the card table helped pay for the food and her rent.

Oh, the kitchen would smell so good with so many aromas wafting through the air! The kitchen was filled with the pungent scents of fried chicken, potato salad, tuna salad, greens, cakes, pies, and an assortment of other foods which Aunt Mamie would sell for fifty cents a plate. Aunt Mamie never ran out of food to feed those folks, no matter how many of them packed into her small apartment, and she would continually fry chicken throughout the night. Those parties would go on until the wee hours of the morning. All night long they ate, played cards, danced, drank, joked, and flirted with each other. But of course, my sisters and I had to go to bed well before the parties had ended, oftentimes before the parties even started. However, sometimes I would sneak out of the bedroom and peek into the party, marveling at how those folks could have so much fun.

On very rare occasions, before the party started, Mama and Aunt Mamie would let us mingle with the adults. On one such occasion I had the opportunity to taste some of the food that one of Aunt Mamie's friends had brought. The woman was Jamaican, and she had made a Jamaican dish made with boiled bananas. She asked me if I wanted to try some of her specialty culinary dish. *Boiled bananas? They had to be good*, I thought, because I loved bananas. And the Jamaican woman assured me that the bananas were delicious, after all it was her native dish. So I began piling my plate full of the bananas. "All right", Aunt Mamie cautioned, "you don't know what it tastes like, and you'd better eat whatever you put on your plate." I reasoned that because I liked bananas, the dish had to be good, so I piled some more on my plate until I had a big plateful of boiled bananas. I eagerly took my first bite, savoring what it would taste like. "Ugh!" I exclaimed when I took my first bite and promptly gagged. The bananas were bitter! So bitter! Aunt Mamie gave me a formidable look of consternation and told me that I had better eat every last bite. And there was Mama, agreeing with Aunt Mamie, conveying with her eyes a whipping if I didn't finish the plateful of boiled bananas. And so, I ate all of the boiled bananas on my plate, because I knew that I would have received a whipping if I didn't. It took me over an hour, but I finished every bite. *Lesson learnt—don't bite off more than you can chew.*

***

Aunt Lillie didn't live with us for too long. She moved out after only a few months. After all, Aunt Mamie's house was like a way station. Kinfolks stayed with her just long enough until they could find a place of their own.

***

After staying with Aunt Mamie for what seemed like a year, Mama moved her family to our own apartment. That was the first of many moves. I remember moving a succession of times. From one stinking hole-in-the-wall to another. At one place, I remember many frightening nights in bed of peering up at the ceiling looking up at the rats looking down on me through the holes in the ceiling, petrified that the rats would jump down and attack me.

At another place, my siblings and I made a game of killing the mice that roamed so freely in our apartment. We would see a mouse at one end of the room, take careful aim, and throw a hard shoe at it. And whack! *Eek-eek-eek,* the mouse would scream in its pathetic, shrill voice, mortally wounded. Desperately trying to hold on to its little life and the entire time running, looking for a place to die. I actually got quite good at killing those mice. Maybe that's why I wasn't afraid of mice like so many other young girls and women.

Most places we moved to had very little heat in the wintertime, and our family had to huddle around coal stoves and free-standing heaters for warmth. And, at every place we moved to, the cockroaches were permanent, non-rent paying, free-loading, crumb-snatching co-tenants.

In one building, we had to share the bathroom with three other tenants on the floor. The bathroom had one little light at the top of the ceiling that was often not working because it had blown out. Other times, there was no light bulb because one of the other tenants had stolen it for use in their own apartment. The landlord was one of those typical slum landlords who very rarely visited the apartment building except to collect his rent. Since he was not there that often, he did not notice that the light bulb was often blown or missing. And if he did notice, he didn't care. And none of the tenants, including my mother, felt compelled to replace a blown or missing light bulb because that was the landlord's job. It was hard enough trying to pay rent without supplying the building with light bulbs. The tenants we shared the bathroom with were so very revolting. Pissing and shitting in the bathtub, or on the floor, oftentimes because the toilet wasn't working. Other times, they did so just because they were nasty. We would never take a bath in the bathtub because it was so filthy that it couldn't be cleaned, even though my mother futilely tried to do so when we first moved into that building. Other than to relieve ourselves, we never used that bathroom.

We washed our faces and brushed our teeth over the kitchen sink. We used a large tin washtub placed in the middle of the kitchen to bathe in. My mother would heat water on the stove and pour it into the washtub, in which everyone would bathe. There was an order to the baths in the tin tub. One by one, we would haunch our little bodies into the tub while Mama leaned over and washed us. The youngest would bathe first, then the older ones, and then my mother. Even bathing in dirty water was preferable to bathing in that foul tub in the floor's bathroom.

We didn't have front or backyards to play in. Wherever we moved, my siblings and I played in the alleys. Some of the alleys were clean, with very little automobile traffic. So it was a lot of fun playing in those. One alley, though, in particular, I remember because of all the broken glass and debris. We had to be extra careful playing in that alley lest we get hurt. Many times we preferred to play inside rather than taking a chance falling on some broken glass in that alley.

We mostly lived in rundown buildings in impoverished communities. One dilapidated building to another to another. I can't remember how many times we moved because we moved so often. *Lesson learnt—life is a process of constant change. You'd better make the best of it.*

***

Somewhere, in between moving from place to place, Mama had another child, a boy named Robert. To me, he just came from out of nowhere. And my sister, Edna, had a baby girl. Edna was only fifteen when she had the baby.

***

When I was about seven years old, I asked Mama about my father. For the most part, she didn't give me too much information about him. She told me his name and that she did not know where he lived. He had moved somewhere else in Mississippi shortly after I was born. She also told me that I had a brother who was in the army and gave me his address. (Wonder where she got that from?) I was thrilled to learn that I had an older brother and promptly sat down and wrote him a letter and gave it to my mother to mail. I never ever got a response from him. But I always wondered about my father and brother and, throughout my life, yearned to meet them. Years later I would learn that my mother had given me the wrong name and wrong address of my brother, which is why he never received the letter, if, in fact, she had even mailed it. And, truth be told, Mama had given me the wrong name of my father.

***

My mother was a religious fanatic, or so it seemed to me. She was extremely religious and strict in my upbringing, having a tendency not to trust me as far as life outside the church was concerned. Mama really didn't trust people outside the church too much anyway, feeling that much of mankind consisted of unsaved heathens. As long as Mama kept me in church or associated with people in the church, everything was okay. In fact, half of my adolescent life was spent in church (where most of the heathens that my mother so greatly feared hung out). We went to church all day on Sundays, from Sunday School through morning service through afternoon service through evening service; on Wednesday evenings for mid-week prayer service; on Thursdays for choir rehearsal; and on Saturdays for Red Circle and Sunshine Band. I went to Vacation Bible School two weeks of every summer, from 10:00 a.m. to 3:00 p.m. Vacation Bible School, Red Circle, and Sunshine Band were fun activities for me because we played games, did arts and crafts, and learned Christian songs. Besides, I really did not understand what the preacher was talking about during church service and was clueless about the meaning of prayer service. But each night, I routinely said my prayers by rote before getting into bed. "*Now I lay me down to sleep. I pray the Lord my soul to keep. If I should die before I wake, I pray the Lord my soul to take.*" "*Our Father, who art in heaven...*"

Every Sunday the church's families would bring food they had prepared from home and share with other church members after morning service and before the afternoon service began. The church basement became one big cafeteria. Some families would cook meats, others vegetables, and others desert. It was as though we were one big happy family sharing a communal meal. After eating our meal, I and the other children would go outside and play until it was time to go into the afternoon service. We would jump rope, play tag and hopscotch, and sneak to the candy store across the street.

I joined the church when I was almost eight years old. When I went to the front row of the church to join during the invitational hymn, the pastor asked me why I wanted to join the church. My confessional statement was, "It's fun to join the church." After all, I reasoned, it was fun playing with my friends, Vacation Bible School, Sunshine Band, and Red Circle.

The pastor looked at me somewhat puzzled. He peered down over his thick glasses at my little body and asked me if I loved the Lord and had I accepted Jesus Christ as my Savior. "Yes," I replied, completely clueless as to what he meant by either question. But my mother was real happy that I had joined the church and was "saved" and became baptized, thereby earning me a place of eternal life in heaven.

During Sunday morning services, I would watch a little old lady, who appeared to be at least sixty years old, jump the pews and incessantly, in a loud, piercing voice, shout, "Hallelujah! Thank you Jesus!" Of course, I had no idea of who this Jesus was, other than the picture of a pale white man with a long beard that hung in the church sanctuary. But, most of all, what mystified me was that that little old lady never missed her footing. She would jump from one pew over to the other, landing solidly on her feet on each pew and then jumping over to another without ever missing her footing. Mama said that the woman was in the "Holy Spirit" and that nothing could harm her while she was in the "Spirit." Other fascinations for me were the little old women who often shouted and wailed during the service. "Oh Lawdy, Lord Jesus, help me, Lawdy, Lord Jesus," they would shout, looking upward toward the ceiling as if looking to heaven, while flailing their arms about them. Others would faint, while those sitting by them would hurriedly scoot out of their way while the ushers ran to put smelling salts under their noses and fan them; some would run around the perimeters of the sanctuary like wild horses in a stampede, only stopping when they had exhausted themselves. I would curiously look at them. *"They must have the Holy Spirit, too,"* I reasoned. But I had no idea about what this Holy Spirit was. *Lesson learnt—the Holy Spirit must be a powerful thing. It can make you do irrational, unexplainable things. Better not mess with it!*

***

Around the time that I turned nine years old, my mother Cora became romantically involved with a man named Carl whom, to my great dismay, she later married. Although he seemed to try to be nice to Cora's children, there was just something about 'that man' that I just didn't like. I couldn't quite put my finger on it, quite the contrary; he was kind to the point of being suspect, like he had an ulterior motive. He was dark-skinned, short stature of medium build, with a slick hairdo, thin lips, and quiet spoken. And he walked around the house too quietly, his feet never making a sound, like he was trying to sneak up on you. He was a sharp dresser, with his suits, shoes, and hats all matching. He often paid more attention to his clothing than to his stepchildren and the children that he and Cora would have. His very eyes bespoke evil, shifty piercing steely brown almost inhuman eyes. In many ways, he reminded me of the caricatures of the devil I had seen in the Bible pictures. Only he was black instead of red. And he didn't have a tail, and his ears weren't pointed. But he was the devil personified, nevertheless. And I was mightily scared of him. And I made it a point to stay out of Carl's way lest I should incur his wrath and cause him to spew fire and brimstone on me from his devil-like mouth.

***

In the summer of my tenth year, Grandma Hattie visited with Cora and her other children in Chicago. Grandma Hattie offered me the chance to go live Down South with her and Grandpa Malone. I was elated! I Jumped at the chance to live with Grandma Hattie and Grandpa Malone and to get away from 'that man' I didn't like. I was also thrilled that I'd be able to once again see my godparents whom I loved so very much.

After a two-week stay, Grandma Hattie and I took the train Down South, the Hummingbird, a gigantic, pretty train, with gray and red stylish decor throughout. I had never been on a train before. So much room! Unlike the cramped bus I had rode Up North on. I could run and skip up and down the aisles and play with the other kids. I was having so much fun that I never noticed how long the ride took. Mama had packed us a lunch of crispy fried chicken, white bread, apples and bananas, and melt-in-your-mouth pound cake. It was so good. When we were halfway to Natchez, in Nashville, we had to change cars.

"Why do we have to change cars, Grandma Hattie? Why can't we stay up here? I like my seat."

"Don't ask so many questions, child," Grandma Hattie replied. "We just have to move to the back of the train."

I thought that it was a little strange that only the Negroes had to move to the last car.

I knew nothing about racism in the South and that at Nashville we were crossing the Mason-Dixie line, officially entering the South where Jim Crow segregation was rigidly enforced. *Lesson re-learnt— racism still exists.*

***

My year Down South was one of the best years of my life! Once again, I found myself in a situation in which I was the only child and loved to death, this time by two sets of parents—my grandparents and my godparents. I was loved so much by them that my cousins were resentful of my special status and would often call me spoiled. But I knew that they were just jealous because they had to share everything with their siblings and I didn't have to share anything with anyone. And I loved and cherished every moment of it. And to my great delight, my grandparents now had an indoor toilet.

My grandfather was an old-fashioned, down-home, hell-fire-and-brimstone Baptist preacher, a strict disciplinarian, a mean, foreboding man, and sometimes just a downright ogre. Although he never spanked me, I was so scared of him that I didn't even dare to *think* anything wrong around him. He was tall, husky, and jet-black, with dark wavy hair. Good hair, as they used to call it. He was part Indian, so I was told, with high cheekbones. An avid wrestling fan, he would often watch wrestling matches until the wee hours of the morning. Sometimes, before bedtime, he would let me watch the wrestling matches with him. I was appalled by the violence, the viciousness, and the "maim-and-destroy" mind-set of the wrestlers. I would flinch each time one of the wrestlers was thrown across the ring and jumped upon and mauled by the other wrestlers. But, for some reason, my grandfather, the "do unto others as you would have them do unto you" and the "God don't like ugly," hell-fire-and-brim-stone preacher, took an open and obvious delight in the brutal violence of these antics, often yelling to his favorite wrestler to kill the other guy, which really conflicted with my concept of doing unto others what you would have them do unto you. *Lesson learnt—sometimes good people can like bad things.*

***

Grandma Hattie began each day by drinking a cup of hot sugared water. A petite, slim, cream-colored, soft-spoken woman, Grandma Hattie worked as a domestic for the white folks and would often bring home goodies from their houses. Little Debbie's. Pound cakes. Hostess Twinkies. And leftover meat and other foods that we could never afford.

Life had aged Grandma Hattie, and she looked much older than her years, having gotten married at the tender age of thirteen and birthing eight children. In fact, she used to be the babysitter for Grandpa Malone's first wife. When she married him, she took on the additional responsibility of raising the four children from his previous marriage.

Grandma Hattie *loved* me and showed that love in every way she could. She often scrimped, sacrificed, and saved to provide some of the nicer things of life that all little girls wanted: pretty shoes and dresses, dolls, candy, and ice cream. Even when she scolded me, Grandma Hattie spoke to me in gentle, even tones, never once raising her voice or yelling.

Best of all, I had the chance to visit with my godparents on a regular basis. On Saturday afternoons, I would walk the few blocks to their house to spend time with them. Godmother Mary had aged so much! Godfather Wilmer had become stooped over, beginning to bald and was going deaf. It didn't matter. I loved being around them and spending time with Richard, my favorite god-brother, who was a few years older than me. The dogs had died since I left five years ago to go Up North. The chickens and pigs were gone. The backyard was barren, no longer flourishing with the vegetables and beautiful, vibrant multicolored flowers. But none of that mattered. All that mattered was that I could, once again, be with them, sleep in my poster bed, and experience their total unconditional love.

We all went to the same church, my grandparents, godparents, aunts, uncles, and cousins. It was very much a family church. And my grandfather was a minister of the church. As far as church went, I had to once again go through the same familiar routine: Sunday School, morning service, afternoon service, Baptist Training Union, and evening service, the weekday choir rehearsals and the midweek service. But, for some reason, I didn't mind. I was happy and carefree, playing with my countless cousins and newfound friends and being surrounded by so much love. *Lesson learnt—unconditional love has no time limits. It's always there.*

***

When I enrolled in school that September, I was not as warmly received as I thought I should have been. My teacher, Mrs. Hatch, called me "that gurl from Up North," as though she resented me having lived in the North and was somewhat openly contemptuous of me, making snide, subtle derisive comments in front of the class to me, like "Yeah, you think you so smart." I knew that I had to be on my best behavior with her and so did my best to have Mrs. Hatch accept me. I turned in homework assignments quickly, with no mistakes. I often raised my hand to answer questions and answered them correctly. I modeled good behavior to the other students. Although Mrs. Hatch was initially very reserved, cold, and evil-natured toward me, in a few months she warmed up to me. She began to openly admire my intelligence and quick wit, so much so that I became known as the "teacher's pet." I got to sit in the front of the classroom where all the smart kids sat. I helped Mrs. Hatch grade the homework papers and even got to run errands for her.

That "gurl from Up North" was in the same classroom as my most favorite cousin, Wendell, who would often entreat me to cheat on English and math tests for him. But I refused to help him cheat because I didn't want to get caught and I didn't want to do anything that would raise Mrs. Hatch's ire and cast me in an unfavorable light. I was crazy about Mrs. Hatch, too. Mrs. Hatch was the only teacher I had ever had who took a personal interest in me. Up North, I was one of the many students in a classroom. Down South, I was a special, highly prized, high-achieving, and highly favored student.

***

On my very first excursion into "town" with my cousins, I boarded the city bus in my usual manner. I sat in the front, close to the bus driver, as my mother had taught me to do for safety reasons. Wendell and my other cousins immediately went to the back of the bus, as was their custom. "Come back here, Mai, with us," Wendell called to me from his back seat.

"Why? I like it up here."

After several futile attempts to get me to move to the back of the bus, Wendell, hoping to lessen the painful ramifications of my adamant refusal to sit in the back of the bus, in a loud beseeching voice, explained to the white bus driver, "You have to excuse her, Suh. She from The North. She don't know no better".

Having been raised in The North, I really didn't know better. I didn't know anything about segregation and how Negroes were supposed to sit in the back of the bus to defer to white folks. And I very seldom saw any white folks anyway. The only white folks I had ever encountered at that point in my life were my school teachers, who seemed to be from another world. My world consisted of my neighborhood, family, and church, all of whom were Negroes.

On my excursion to town, I once again saw the For Whites Only and For Colored Only signs at the water fountains and bathrooms. "Why is that, Wendell? We don't have any signs like that in Chicago."

"That's just the way it is," Wendell replied with a sigh of resignation.

Having been raised in the South, he knew the Jim Crow rules and the ramifications of breaking them. *Lesson learnt—racism is alive and well, and you better not cross the lines.*

***

After I had been south for a few months, I noticed that several times a week my older cousins and other older men and women would be picked up in a red pick-up truck at daybreak and taken somewhere, returning late in the evening. "Where do you be going?," I asked my older cousin, Sam, one day.

"Picking cotton."

"Oooh, can I go? That sounds like fun!"

He thought about it real hard for a moment and replied. "No, you're too little. The work is too hard for you."

I always regretted not being able to go pick cotton. I thought it would be such fun. I had absolutely no idea about picking cotton, how grueling it was, and the cruel, demeaning, and exploitive role it had played in the lives of Black folks in the South.

***

I loved being "underfoot" around my older adult kinfolks. I was not allowed to participate in their conversations because they said that children should be seen and not heard. But they had such juicy gossip! When they discussed something they considered "adult" and not suitable for a child's ears, they would speak in hushed voices and spell out the words. I didn't mind them spelling out the words because, unbeknownst to them, I was an excellent speller and knew how to use phonics to sound out the words. I did, however, mind them speaking in hushed tones though because I couldn't always hear what was being said. On one occasion, my aunt and grandmother talked in really hushed voices about someone being "r-a-p-e-d". *R-a-p-e-d, Raped,* I thought, *what is raped?* All I knew was that it had to be something bad because of the strained expressions on their faces and the consternation and angst in their voices. So the next day I went and looked it up in the dictionary at school. It had something to do with a forced penetration of a woman, but I didn't know what that meant. Penetrating what? Another time I heard something about the Ku Klux Klan burning down someone's house in retaliation for being "uppity." *What is the Ku Klux Klan? And why would they do that?* So, I looked up Ku Klux Klan in the dictionary, but it wasn't there. So I figured that the Ku Klux Klan must be a local group, a local group of mean-spirited people. *Lesson learnt—Negroes better "stay in their place" or suffer for breaking Jim Crow rules.*

***

When I was not busy being underfoot, I was happily enjoying life with my family and newfound friends. Yes, I have some very fond memories of that year. Wrapping the flag pole on May Day with long strands of multicolored crepe paper. *Here we go round the mulberry bush, the mulberry bush, the mulberry bush. Here we go round the mulberry bush so early in the morning.* Halloween, in which my cousins and I ran up and down the dark streets trick or treating, scaring the hell out of people and being scared the hell back. Wendell finding a turtle's nest by the swamp and boiling the turtle's eggs for a scrumptious treat. Spending time with my best friend, Patricia, with whom I spent many sleepovers, playing with our homemade dolls and fantasizing about the families and houses we would have when we grew up.

Swinging on the huge tire hanging from the gigantic willow tree in my grandparents' front yard, trying to reach the sky. The banana trees and grapevines and all the rows and rows of fruits and vegetables in my grandparents' huge garden. Sucking on the succulent "bullets" that grew in the garden. Seeing my grandfather hoe his garden with his mule. *Whoa, mule! Giddye on up, mule!* Listening to my grandfather preach one of his many hell and damnation, fire and brimstone sermons. Watching Miss Letty spit snuff clear across the road. Sam falling down into an outhouse and being hosed down by his mother Muh-dear to rid his body of the stinking shit he had fallen into. And looking for my mysterious older brother whom they said sometimes returned to the city to visit some of his friends and relatives.

I remember many days playing with my cousins in an empty lot, adjacent to my aunt Muh-dear's house, on which a new house was being built. One day the grass was wet and slippery because of a recent rain.

On that day, while playing a game of chase on that wet grass, I slipped and fell, hitting my head hard against the corner of a stack of bricks that were being used to build the house. I screamed and hollered bloody murder and had quite a gash in the top of my head, with lots of blood oozing out of it. "*Oh, Muh-dear, Muh-dear. Mai done hurt herself! Come look at that hole in her head!*", Wendell yelled to his mother, while taking me back to his house.

"Hush, Chile. Come here, Mai. Let me look at it."

Wendell just kept frantically hollering, "Oh, look at that big hole in her head!"

Muh-dear examined the gaping hole in my head, cut the hair off surrounding it, and proceeded to pour alcohol in the hole and taped it up with gauze and a big Band-Aid. "You'll be all right. Now go lay down."

"But, Muh-dear, I need to go to the hospital. I'm bleeding. My head hurts."

Still crying and whimpering, I complied with my aunt's order. And I was all right. The hole in my head closed over a period of a few days. I never could understand, though, why Muh-dear wouldn't take me to the hospital. After all, my mother would have immediately taken me to a hospital. I didn't know, at the time, that Muh-dear had no medical coverage and that she couldn't afford to pay a hospital bill. *Lesson learnt—you don't always need a doctor. The body can heal itself.*

Later, in my adult years, I would say that I was crazy, affected, because of that hole in my head.

***

Toward the end of the year of my return to the South, my grandmother announced that she was going Up North to visit her children. Did I want to go with her? *Oh, yeah!* Although I really hadn't given too much thought to my mother, sisters, and brother, I suddenly realized that I did, indeed, miss them. It would be good to see them again. I talked to my mother who asked me if I wanted to stay Down South or come back to live with my family. I realized that I had really missed my family and told my mother that I wanted to come back home. My mother asked me again and told me that I couldn't change my mind. But I was so excited about seeing my mother, sisters, and brother again that I said that I was sure that I wanted to return home. So, Grandma Hattie and I packed our bags and shoebox lunch and went Up North on the Hummingbird. We boarded at the back of the train. But for some reason, when we arrived in Nashville, we moved up to the front of the train.

***

Upon my return to Chicago, I learned that, once again, Mama had moved. To my surprise, I was really happy to see my mother, sisters Berniece and Edna, and brother Robert and my niece. I greeted each one of them with big hugs and kisses. I romped and played with them and shared my Down South experiences with them. 'That man,' Carl, my mother's boyfriend, was still around. But even that couldn't spoil my joy. Mama also had another baby while I was Down South, a boy named Reginald.

After I had been home only one day, Mama asked me if I wanted to go back Down South with Grandma Hattie. Of course not! I was having too much fun with my sisters and brothers and little niece. Mama asked me if I was sure about my decision not to return to the South. Sure, I'm sure!

I had been home for about one week before 'that man' started getting on my nerves. Although I tried to like him because he was my mother's friend, I really, really didn't like him at all. He was always looking at me somewhat lecherously. I tried to get along with him, but in most cases, I would tiptoe around him. In my own childish divination, I perceived something truly evil, even Satanic, about that man. He was so sinister, so evil, that he made me extremely uncomfortable. So uncomfortable that I wanted to go back Down South with my grandmother.

***

After a visit of two weeks, it was time for Grandma Hattie to return home. I begged to go back with her.

"No," Mama said, "I asked you twice. Now it's too late."

I pleaded, I begged. I cried genuine colossal tears. I wanted desperately to return Down South with my grandmother so that I wouldn't have to be around 'that man'. I had an evil foreboding about him. Something just wasn't right, and I didn't want to be around to find out what it was. I fell to the floor, in heartbreaking wails, tearing at my mother's skirt tail begging to go back Down South with Grandma Hattie. All to no avail. It was set in stone. My grandmother was returning Down South the next day without me. Tearfully, I, with the rest of the family, accompanied my grandmother to the train station for her return trip home. As I watched her board the train, the reality of my situation set in. *Oh no, I'm doomed.*

I had to settle down to a new life. I was no longer the only child, the favored one, the darling of my grandmother's and godparents' eyes, and the envy of my cousins. And I certainly was not the apple of my mother's eye. Now, I had become one of the few, instead of the only one, and within a few short years of my mother's copious fertile years, one of the many.

***

Before long, I learned that Edna and Mama were going to have another baby. This time both had boys. I had no clue as to how Edna or Mama got those babies. All I knew was that the babies were cute and cuddly and that I had a lot of fun with them, holding, hugging, and kissing them. When Mama found out that Edna was pregnant with her second child, she was furious and issued an ultimatum to her.

"You have to get married. You're not going to lay up on me and have babies!"

A few months before Mama married 'that man,' Edna moved out of the house. So Edna, at the tender age of seventeen, and Kelvin, eight years her senior, got married. By this time, I had a little bit of an idea of how Edna had become pregnant. She had been with a boy. And she had raised her skirt. That's how she got pregnant! Cause Mama said, "If you be with dem boys and raise your skirt, you gonna get pregnant." I resolved then and there that I would never be with any boys and certainly not raise my skirt or dress around them.

When I registered for school that fall after my arrival back Up North, I was supposed to have been in the sixth grade because I had completed the fifth grade Down South. However, the principal tried to get me to repeat the fifth grade because I had completed it Down South in a so-called inferior educational system. For the principal had been brainwashed into believing that southern schools were inferior. I boo-hooed and boo-hooed. "No, Mama, no," I screamed, "I don't want to be put back."

"*Well, Mai, they said they have to put you back. You have to repeat fifth grade.*"

"But I know all of the fifth grade stuff. I'm ready for the sixth grade. Besides, only dummies get put back."

For I considered myself to be smart, and being put back a grade was the ultimate humiliation, tantamount to death. In fact, I didn't just consider myself to be smart; I *knew* I was smart because Mrs. Hatch had told me so on many occasions. I always passed every test with flying colors, even before I attended school Down South. Oh, no, it would never do to be put back. The decision to put me back a grade didn't sit well with my mother either, for Mama knew that I was an extremely bright, inquisitive, quick-witted, and intelligent child. But she didn't know what to do; the principal had given the order and that was that.

"Mama, tell them to give me a test. The test will show that I can do the work." I relished the opportunity to show them folks that I was no dummy. But the principal denied Mama's request to give me the sixth grade entrance exam. I prayed and prayed and prayed because the principal was like a rock that would not be moved. Mama went back to the school several times to appeal to the principal in an effort to get him to change his mind. On her last visit to the principal's office, she resolutely demanded that I be given a test to determine which grade level I should be in. Reluctantly, the principal relented. *Must be those prayers*, I thought and thanked God for the opportunity to show the principal that I should not have to repeat fifth grade.

My mother and I looked forward to the test day. That morning, when we arrived at the school, the principal tried to talk me out of taking the test, "Just go ahead and repeat the grade."

But I was adamant. "I'm ready for the test," I said.

The principal took me to an empty classroom, gave me the sixth grade entrance exam and the instructions, explaining that I had an hour to answer all the questions, and then left the room and closed the door. I studied the questions and quickly answered them. In short order, I was finished and took the completed test to the principal's office where my mother was waiting.

"Are you sure you're finished?", the principal asked incredulously. "You have thirty more minutes to complete this test."

"No, I'm finished," I replied.

"Well, we'll let you know the results by tomorrow."

The next day, the principal called my mother. With a voice of total astonishment and amazement, he informed my mother that not only had I tested at grade level, but I had tested well above grade level, earning a promotion to the next half-grade if I so wished. But Mama and I were so happy that I could enter into my rightful grade that we declined the offer of the grade promotion. *Ha! So much for the inferior schools of the South!* I thought, "Mrs. Hatch would be proud me." And so, that fall, I entered school in my rightful grade. *Lesson learnt—believe in yourself and follow through on that belief no matter what others may think or say.*

***

Shortly after I passed the sixth grade entrance exam, our family moved again. The place to which we moved was a coach house that had an oversized yard behind the main house. It was the first time ever that we had a yard to play in. No more playing in alleys littered with debris and incalculable bits of broken glass. Berniece and I would play for hours in that huge yard. We made up a ditty about our landlady Mrs. Jennie. Mrs. Jennie had a gargantuan butt. She had the biggest boody that we had ever seen. It had to be the biggest one in the whole wide world! It was ever so round and lumpy. I didn't know that those lumpy bumps were called cellulite. I just called it lumpy. Ms. Jennie's butt shook like Jell-O whenever she walked, and it had to be the size of an eighteen-wheeler truck tire and just as round. So Berniece and I concocted a ditty about Mrs. Jennie's butt while doing a rumba type of dance. "*Jennie the hut, with the big fat butt! Jennie the hut, with the big fat butt!*" thrusting our diminutive hips out on and accentuating the words "hut" and "butt." For hours on end, in the daylight and at night, we would sing and dance our song. It was so much fun. "Jennie the hut, with the big fat butt! Jennie the hut, with the big fat butt! Jennie the hut, with the big fat butt! Jennie the hut, with the big fat butt!" Of course, we never let our mother or Mrs. Jennie hear us. For we knew, that if they did, we would get the whipping of a lifetime for mocking an adult. But we did share our ditty and dance with our brother Robert, who enjoyed it just as much and often sang and fervently danced our ditty with us.

Over the course of time, I became thoroughly indoctrinated with the "Spirit of God," having been in church most days and nights of the week for my young life. I really didn't mind going to church so much. I had a lot of friends there, and we often played together during and between services. We would frequently sneak out of the sanctuary under the pretense of having to go to the bathroom. Once downstairs, we would dart to the corner store and spend part of our offering money on candy and chips. Most times, our parents didn't catch us playing hooky from church, but when they did! Whippings and pinchings were administered with the vengeance of God by our parents.

Berniece and I often played "church" together in the big front yard of the coach house in which we lived. We would sing and shout; one would fan the other as we were having our shouting spells, jumping and falling out of our seats, mimicking the church women who were "overcome by the 'Spirit'."

One day out of the clear blue sky, I felt that I had a calling from God to preach a sermon. It was as if I had been "divinely touched by the finger of God," commanding me to preach a sermon to all those who passed by. This was to be my first and only sermon. Berniece was not present. Neither was Robert. And neither was anyone else. All by myself, alone in that big front yard (my church building), I preached my sermon. For over twenty minutes I preached about hell and damnation, fire and brimstone, the eternal burning of bodies in hell, and the evils of Satan; the pearly gates and the golden streets of heaven, flowing with milk and honey where the saints would praise God all day and all night; and all of the things I heard the preachers preach. I mimicked their mannerisms. I ah-hummed. I sweated. I wiped my brow with a big white handkerchief. I shouted, fanatically jumping up and down. I beseeched the Lord not to "Pass Me By" and sang "Come to Jesus" as my invitational hymn, imploring all who heard my sermon while walking by to accept the Lord Jesus Christ as their Savior so that they wouldn't be doomed to eternal damnation. I extended my hand, as I had seen the preachers do, entreating all who passed by me to join my church. All the things I had seen and heard in church. Passersby curiously looked at me; some shaking their heads, others smiling at that young girl who was obviously possessed. But none stopped to join my church and get their souls saved.

***

Within a year of my return to the North, Mama married 'that man.' Because Mama was such a church fanatic, she preached to him constantly about his sinful ways of drinking, smoking, running the streets, and playing the blues until he "repented" and joined the church. He actually attended services, even joined the Usher Board. They were married in a small ceremony in the pastor's study. Berniece and I shed tears, though not tears of joy. They were tears of apprehension and foreboding about the future ahead with 'that man.' Robert and Reginald didn't have a clue as to what was going on, and Edna wasn't there.

In a strange kind of way, I was glad that they were getting married, because I so badly wanted a father and felt incomplete without one. I would often be envious of my church friends who had fathers. Mama was quite evasive whenever I asked questions about my father. All I knew was the little bit she told me about him: his name (which turned out to be the wrong name) and that he had left her years ago. I often fantasized what it would be like to have a father. I even fantasized that the church's pastor was my father. Cause I really didn't know who my father was or anything about him. So I settled for what I had: fantasies and daydreams. But I never stopped looking for my father and brother, whom I knew so little about.

Although my life upon my return was not too hard, my carefree days were forever gone. I had to assume responsibilities that I had never thought about. I had to babysit my younger siblings and play mother when my mother was not around. And this stepfather of mine would not take the responsibility of helping to raise the kids, not even his own.

My stepfather was working and still going to church. But he loved the blues and would smoke cigars, drink, and often frequent bars, coming home tipsy to drunk. *This is no good*, I thought. And I would redouble my efforts to avoid him. When he drank, which he often did, he would habitually argue with my mother who would not back down from him, which, needless to say, set the stage for many ferocious arguments and subsequent fights.

There was something else about 'that man' that really disturbed me. He would often glance at me in ways that made me uncomfortable and would needlessly, seemingly innocently unintentionally, touch me, often in "no-no" places, like my developing hips and budding breasts. And he would do it only when my mother was not around. And Mama was not around a lot of evenings because she was at church. Wednesday night Bible study; Thursday night choir rehearsal; mid-week evangelizing. "*Hmphh!*", I thought, "*She ought to be here trying to save this sinner who lives in this house and treats us like stray dogs.*"

When the touchings first started, I initially thought that he was finally beginning to like me and to accept me as one of his own children. I was beginning to feel special once again—the cherry of someone's eye. I really didn't know any better. After all, my godfather and uncle often hugged and touched me as demonstrations of their love. I thought that maybe this was the same thing. And so, at first, I didn't protest but rather acquiesced to his initial exploratory touches. Those exploratory touches were of an infrequent nature, maybe every other month or so. When he determined that I was not resistant to his touches, he increased their frequency and the length of the touches, letting his hands linger on my tender "no-no" body parts. Then he began kissing me, quick kisses, on the cheek and on the forehead. By this time, I was beginning to feel ill at ease with his advances but didn't know how to stop them. I didn't know how to tell my mother about it for Mama did not really open up to personal and private conversations with me. In fact, Mama never talked about anything personal with me. Mama did not know how I felt about anything, other than school and church. And more than anything, I dared not tell for fear of having my stepfather getting angry with me and whipping me for telling.

With the touches, I truly became a surrogate mother, an eleven-year-old surrogate mother. Being the oldest, I already had the responsibility of watching after the younger kids in my mother's absence. But now, I was beginning to take on the role of his wife. A role I didn't want. In spite of my desperate need to be loved and cherished, I just really didn't like 'that man.'

In time, he became bolder in his advances toward me. When Mama was in church, as she so often was, he began calling me to his bedroom after I had gotten the kids settled down. He had me lay there on his bed (his and my mama's bed) while his hands roamed and explored my developing body. Sometimes he would just let his hand rest on my thing. This would petrify me so much that all I could do was freeze, paralyzed with fear. I just lay still with my eyes closed in dreadful terror, hoping that it would be over soon. And usually within five minutes, but what seemed to be an hour to me, he had satisfied his lustful meanderings over my body and let me go.

So I redoubled my efforts to make sure that I was never alone but was always with one of my siblings, that one of them would always need my attention. In my own way, I devised every scheme I could think of to avoid him, spending more time helping my brothers and sister do their homework, bathing them, and playing games with them.

Then one night, once again, Mama left us alone to go to church again. As Mama was leaving, I cried out, "Mama, don't go!"

"Why not?", asked Mama.

But I could not give her a reason why, what 'that man' was doing to me in her absence. I was too petrified to tell my mother about 'that man.' I couldn't utter the words to tell my mother what was going on in her household while she was in church praising God instead of protecting her child. And, so, Mama, not hearing a reason from me as to why not to go to church, walked on out the door.

I kept myself as busy as I could with the kids, thinking up stuff for them to do, playing games, cleaning their room, and reading to them, hoping that my mother would come home soon. But Mama was taking too long to come home from church, way too long, much longer than usual, and it was time for the kids to go to bed. After I tucked them in, he called me. "Mai, come here."

I looked to see where his voice was coming from. Oh, no. He was in the bedroom! I cringed by the bedroom door, frightened by the prospect of 'that man' fondling me once more.

"Come here," he said.

He was lying down on the bed wearing only a white T-shirt and white boxers. This was the first time that he had undressed, and I became mightily afraid. I timidly went over to the bed where he was laying down.

"Lay down," he commanded.

I meekly complied with his request. Then began the touching, the stroking. All at once, he put his body squarely on top of me, something he had never done before. Then he put his hand under my dress, started rubbing my little thing with his fingers, and thrust his stinky cigar-tasting tongue deep into my mouth.

I began whimpering and crying. "No! No! No! No!"

"You don't want to do this?", he gruffly asked.

"No," I sobbed, weeping almost uncontrollably.

"You can go then." I hurriedly ran out of the room and strongly resolved to never, never, ever be alone in his presence again, no matter what. And I didn't know how to tell Mama about it, feeling ashamed, as though it were my fault. For in my eyes, my mother did not view me as a child, needing to be loved, talked to, and reassured about life but rather treated me instead like hired help without the pay. Even though I never told my mother about Carl's advances, I felt deep within my heart that my mother just had to know about it. I resented my mother for leaving me alone so often with 'that man.' But I needed not to have worried about him touching me again, for he never once touched me again after that night.

***

I was awfully confused by all of it. My stepfather was nothing like the fathers I and my best friend Patricia had fantasized about. He was a stingy, mean, perverted bastard. He was nothing like my pastor who seemed so nice and kind. He was nothing like Beaver's and Wally's father on *Leave it to Beaver*. They cared about their kids and wouldn't deprive them of life's little pleasures. Beaver's father didn't fondle little girls (at least not on TV). What I had initially thought was a display of love on my stepfather's part was nothing but a lecherous old man getting his jollies. A pedophile.

So I really didn't know what a father's and man's role should be. Nothing jived with what I had read in my storybooks and seen on television, leaving me to further fantasize about the ideal father and ideal man, which accounts for some major problems I had in my relationships with men. *Lesson learnt—all fathers aren't good men; some are just dirty old men.*

***

Later in life, I learned that so many other girls had experiences like mine with their stepfathers and other male relatives. I was not alone, not the only one who had been molested. Some of my girlfriends' testimonies were much worse than mine. A few of my friends told me horrendous stories of their molestations and rape by a relative. By happenstance I read a book, *No More Secrets*, which helped me to understand my stepfather's actions, why I chose to respond as I had, and the choices I made in life as a result of these experiences and the path to healing. *Lesson learnt—don't keep painful experiences to yourself. Others have been through what you're going through.*

***

Thirty-five years later, I would learn that my older sister, Edna, had had the same problems with Carl, which accounted in large part for her promiscuity in her young, teenage years. Edna even slept with a butcher knife under her pillow with the intent of killing him if he approached her bed while she was sleeping. Forty-eight years later, Edna also confirmed that our mother knew about Carl's advances toward us. She even told me that Carl had tried to set her up at the age of sixteen with one of his friends with Mama's consent. He brought one of his lewd friends to the house and openly tried to set him up with Edna, and our mother did nothing about it. I recalled a doctor's visit when I was in my freshman year of high school. Mama took me to the doctor because I kept experiencing constant terrible horrific pains in my side. After examining me, the doctor told me to step outside his office so that he could talk with Mama. I later asked Mama what the doctor said about my pains. Mama replied that there was nothing physically wrong with me and that the pains were psychosomatic. Then the doctor asked her what was going on in her household. Mama didn't tell me what her response was to the doctor. Upon recalling that visit and subsequent conversations with Edna, I, too, became convinced that Mama knew that something was going on with Carl that would cause me to experience such excruciating pain.

***

In our later years conversations, Edna almost cried when she learned that my siblings and I had attended Mama's and Carl's marriage ceremony but she had not because she didn't know about it. Clearly anguished, Edna said, "You all were there? Why didn't she invite me? I was her daughter, too."

I didn't have an answer for her. What could I say? Also, I learned that Mama was even more distant from Edna than she was with me. Edna, also, never enjoyed a healthy mother-daughter relationship. Edna, too, was a surrogate mother, having constantly babysat her younger siblings, which also accounted for the fact that she married young. To get away from Mama and 'that man.' Edna kept a lot of bitterness; she just couldn't shake it loose. Because of the age difference and the fact that she moved away before most of her siblings were born, she was also estranged from her younger brothers and sisters, with the exception of me, only because I used to frequently babysit for her. Edna lived her life as though she had missed out on a lot of her childhood, which, in reality, she did. But she projected her bitterness onto her other brothers and sisters, none of whom appreciated it. She often brought up how she took care of us (because Mama was in church), how she changed our diapers and bathed, fed, and raised us. She felt as though her siblings owed her for that. But it

39

wasn't our fault that Edna had been relegated to such a role. We had nothing to do with it. And, also, we resented her for trying to make us feel guilty about something over which we had no control. And I had to remind Edna on several occasions that I, too, had become the surrogate mother after she left. *Lesson learnt—don't blame others for circumstances over which they have no control.*

***

I did have some good times during those years. When I was in junior high school (the seventh and eighth grades), Mama once again moved to a nicer place. This place, too, was nice. It was so nice, in fact, that Berniece and I made up a short ditty about the address, which we sang and danced to much like the Jennie the hut with the big fat butt ditty. We would sing 4212 South Lunt Street, 4212 South Lunt Street, drawing out the last forty-two twelve South Lunt Street. Over and over we would sing and do our accompanying rumba dance, thrusting our hips out on and accentuating our voices on the word street.

My *best, best* girlfriend's name was Evelyn, and she lived right across the street. We spent many hours together playing with our dolls, talking about life (the very little we knew about it), and talking about the other kids on the block. Evelyn and I went to the same school and had some of the same classes together. We would often study together, helping one another get good grades.

***

Evelyn had a younger sister, Sharon, who was two years younger than her. For some reason, I always picked on Sharon. Not that I didn't like her or anything like that, for she really was a nice girl. I picked on her just because I could. Although Sharon was only a little more than a year younger than me, she was much smaller than me. Maybe that's why, almost daily, I picked on her, hitting her, pushing her, and teasing her. Because she was so small and defenseless, I could take out all of my aggression and frustrations on her. And Evelyn never told me to stop picking on her sister. So, figuring that it was alright with Evelyn, I kept on doing it. On the way to school. From school. While we were playing. Just for the hell of it. Sharon kept on warning me, "You better stop it. One day I'm going to get you back. I'm tired of you messing with me!"

Her words fell on deaf ears. After about six months of being picked on, Sharon told me, once again, not to mess with her. Once more, her words fell on deaf ears, and I began my "messing with Sharon" routine. One day when we were on the way from school, I began messing with Sharon once again, hitting her and shoving her. Sharon spied a two-by-four lying on the ground, picked it up, and started menacingly toward me. "I told you I'm tired of this shit!", she yelled. A crowd of kids eager to see a real down-home fight started gathering around us as Sharon threateningly advanced toward me with her newly found, and definitely threatening, weapon.

I saw the unbridled anger in Sharon's eyes and knew that I was "sho-nuff" for real in trouble. "I was just playing, Sharon. I was just playing!" and began hurriedly backing away.

"Don't play the fuck with me no more," she bellowed. Sharon's defiance certainly earned my respect and fear. And sho-nuff, from that day on, I didn't mess the fuck with her anymore. *Lesson learnt— when someone tells you that they're tired of you messing with them, you'd better believe it.*

***

Most of the neighborhood kids played in the streets together, right in the middle of the street as there was very little traffic. There were a bunch of us—the neighborhood kids. At the age of twelve, I was introduced to a game called Spin the Bottle. This game was most appropriate at that time because I was beginning to discover boys, and my little hormones were starting to kick in (though not for 'that man' that my mother married). In Spin the Bottle, the boys stand on one side of a Coca-Cola bottle and the girls stand on the other side. A boy spins the bottle. If the bottle stops in front of another boy, he loses his turn and another boy spins the bottle. When the bottle stops in front of a girl, the boy spinning the bottle must kiss the girl it stops in front of.

That game was fun! Except when an ugly boy got to kiss me. Nobody wanted the ugly boys to kiss them, but there were some real cute boys on my block. One's name was Elijah, who was so-o-o cute, with hazel brown eyes, wavy hair, caramel-colored skin, a prominent aquiline nose, and thin lips. But Bay-Bay! He was The One. All of the girls wanted him to be their boyfriend. He was so much more handsome than Elijah. He was tall, had pretty light brown eyes, and good hair (but not as good as Elijah's). But he had something else called sex appeal, which we really didn't understand, but it worked. He was real soft-spoken, and all the girls would swoon when he paid them some attention and hoped that the bottle would land in front of them when he spun it.

Another game we played together was the pretend game of House. We played House under the back porches of one of the kids' house. The game required that it be played in utmost secrecy because if one of our parents ever caught us playing House, we were sure that we would be murdered, dismembered, and sent straight to hell with all its fire and brimstone to burn eternally.

In House, one of the girls would play the mother, and one of the boys would play the father; the others would take turns playing the children. We rotated who would play mother and father and children. We would pretend that we were all one big happy family. The "mother" would help the children get ready for school, fix their breakfasts and lunches, and send them off to "school." The "father" would get ready to go to work, and the "mother" would kiss him goodbye. When he returned from "work" (about five minutes later, the same time that the other kids returned from "school"), the "mother" would have their make-pretend dinner prepared for them. They would put the kids to bed and then retire to bed. That was the part that I liked. Because the "mother" and "father" would kiss each other "good night," at which point the game would end.

One time when it was my turn to play the "mother," Bay-Bay played the "father." I couldn't believe my good luck! For that meant that Bay-Bay would have to kiss me. When he kissed me goodbye to go to "work," I almost fainted! He hugged me and leaned his tall, firm body over and kissed me. His hug was so firm, and his lips were so juicy and soft. And he smelled so good, for he was freshly bathed. That kiss was so gooooood. And when he returned from "work," the "family" ate dinner and went to bed. Bay-Bay and I then lay down on the ground (our bed) and he hugged and kissed me good night. That kiss was even better than the morning kiss! Oh, how my hot body juices were flowing! It blew my twelve-year-old mind. It was nothing reprehensible like when my stepfather touched me. Bay-Bay's light touch made me feel on fire, like a flaming torch. And he even put his tongue, ever so lightly, in my mouth. It was like a silk cloth tantalizing, teasing, and exploring every sensation in my mouth. It was an experience I never forgot.

Evelyn and I spent many hours talking about Bay-Bay. Not that he was interested in either one of us, but it was fun talking about him anyway.

***

I graduated from junior high school with honors. I really loved junior high. I met a lot of friends and got to be teacher's pet with a lot of my teachers. I joined the junior high choir and band and received a scholarship to take private dramatic arts lessons. I and my siblings regularly attended after school programs at the neighborhood Garfield Park Recreation Center. The Recreation Center offered classes in sewing, art, swimming, basketball, homework assistance, dance, and acting. I participated in as many classes as I could, including acting, dancing, and sewing. I really enjoyed those times spent at the Recreation Center, even though I had to take my siblings with me. At least we weren't in the same classes.

My most favorite junior high school teacher was also the meanest teacher in the school, Mr. Hill, an eighth grade teacher. Back then, teachers could exercise corporal punishment, something Mr. Hill relished. Students could expect to be "paddled" on their rumps whenever they were late or got caught talking in class or chewing gum. The only way not to be paddled was to pay a five-cent fine.

Because most of the kids were poor, most did not have the five cents and wound up being paddled, including me. Since I loved to talk in class and was notorious for being late, I was often paddled. It seemed as though Mr. Hill took particular pleasure in paddling me, like he was trying to break my spirit.

One day, Mama had a little extra money and gave us a portion of it. I was ecstatic! After all, it wasn't that often that I had spending money. The most money I received was for church offerings, although most of the time I didn't put all of it in the offering tray. After all, some had to go to the candy store which I and my church friends would frequent between services.

So, on that day, I not only also had enough to buy some potato chips, I had enough to pay Mr. Hill's fine if I was late to class. So I deliberately hung around at Papa Joe's after lunch until the late bell rang. Papa Joe's was the hot dog and hamburger joint directly across the street from the school, where many of my classmates ate lunch. Papa Joe's was most famous for its gigantic brown paper bags of potato chips loaded with hot sauce. Everyone agreed that those were the best chips in the world, certainly in the city of Chicago. And their bag of chips only cost a dime. I took my own sweet time moseying across the street from Papa Joe's to the school, arriving at Mr. Hill's class five minutes after the late bell rang.

I sauntered into the classroom and stubbornly looked at Mr. Hill, who had a salivating, hungry look of anticipation in his eyes as he looked forward to giving me an extra hard paddling because I was so late. When he called me to the front of the room for my paddling (all paddlings were done in the front of the class to cause maximum humiliation), he asked me in his typical all-knowing way if I had the five-cent penalty. He was so used to me saying "no" that he had already picked up the paddle. Without waiting for me to answer, he told me to lean over. I triumphantly looked at him and said, "Mr. Hill, sir, you can't paddle me. I have the money for the fine. Here's my nickel."

Oh, you should have seen the look of dismay and surprise in Mr. Hill's eyes! He was almost speechless. He managed to mutter, "You have the fine?" and like where did you get money from? Just to see the look on his face was worth a thousand nickels. My classmates snickered at Mr. Hill's lost opportunity to do some serious butt whacking. I had a defiant look as I proceeded to my seat. Hmmph! Break my spirit. I don't think so! *Lesson learnt—money can get you out of same painful things.*

***

Eighth grade passed so quickly. Students were deciding which high schools we would attend. Some of my best friends and I were going our separate ways. We would all miss Papa Joe's.

***

Graduation day was approaching. For graduation day, one student would be selected to give the graduation speech. Selection of the student was not based upon grades but upon their oratory skills. All students had the opportunity to audition for the graduation speech. Out of ten students who auditioned, Judy and I were the two finalists selected. I practiced the speech with my dramatic arts teacher, Mrs. Woodson. Since sixth grade, I had been taking dramatic arts lessons (that's what it was called then. I had received a scholarship for the dramatic arts lessons because of my dramatic arts skills I demonstrated in the Recreation Center's free lessons which Mrs. Woodson taught. Now it's called acting lessons). Mrs. Woodson was a tall, stately, somewhat husky woman whose diction and grammar were absolutely impeccable. Man, could she enunciate and pronunciate her words! In private lessons, she would endlessly drill her students on proper pronunciation, using tongue twisters like "She sells sea shells by the sea shore" and "Betty Botter had some butter." "But", she said, "this butter's bitter. If I bake this bitter butter, it would make my batter bitter. But a bit of better butter, that would make my batter better." Another tongue twister was "How much wood would a woodchuck chuck if a woodchuck could chuck wood? He would chuck, he would as much as he could and chuck as much wood as a woodchuck could if a woodchuck could chuck wood."

Mrs. Woodson felt that I had the potential to be an actress and was always casting me in the many recitals that her drama troupe would perform throughout the city at various churches, park districts, and other venues. Once a year she would host a talent show in which her students would perform their best pieces. I always got a lot of applause for my poems and monologues, especially for my performance of *The Creation* by John Weldon Johnson. "And God stepped out on space... Amen!", I would enunciate in a booming voice. I would put such feeling and spirit into my dramatizations, remembering to use my hands and facial gestures as well as body language, always receiving loud applause at the end of my speech.

However, when I practiced my graduation speech, Mrs. Woodson insisted that I use a flat tone of voice, with no fluctuations or hand gestures. Well, this went against everything I had been taught about dramatic arts! So I played along with Mrs. Woodson, practicing the speech the way she wanted it done, knowing that when the audition came I would do it my way. On the day of the audition, Judy went first, reciting the speech in a monotonous voice. *So dull, so boring,* I thought as I listened to Judy, *Almost put me to sleep.* When it was my turn to go to the podium to deliver the speech, I put a lot of animation and voice fluctuations between high pitches and low tones. I put so much feeling into that speech, like I was delivering a Sermon on the Mount. *I know I have it,* I triumphantly thought as I went to my seat. *I was so much better than Judy.* After a few minutes, the judges announced their selection. It was Judy! How could they?? That experience taught me a valuable lesson. *Lesson learnt—listen to the experts.*

***

My graduation day was so exciting. I felt like I was on cloud nine. I was ecstatic as I walked down the aisle to receive my diploma. Some of the girls didn't graduate because they were pregnant. But I had learned at an early age to avoid those boys and not to raise my skirt. On graduation night, my favorite uncle, Uncle Harry, took me and Mama for dinner to Mrs. Little Jack's, which was then one of the best and most expensive restaurants on the west side of Chicago. It was truly elegant. The ambiance. Sparkling white linen tablecloths. Lit candles on each table. Soft lighting throughout the restaurant. Expensive carpeting. Fine sterling silverware. Linen napkins. There were three forks by each plate setting, although I only used one and wondered what the other two were for. There were waiters serving my table, attending to my every wish. I felt so special. After all, the most "eating out" I had done was at Papa Joe's hot dog stand. And Uncle Harry told me that I could order anything I wanted! He thought enough of me to treat me to the very best. That's how my husband is going to treat me when I grow up I thought. Real special. Real Mistake.

***

The summer after I graduated from junior high right before I started attending high school, when I was twelve, we moved into the projects. I said my goodbyes to Evelyn who was going to a different high school. I never saw her or Sharon again after we moved. I never saw Bay-Bay or Elijah again. That chapter of my life was closed. *Lesson learnt—life goes on, cherish the memories.*

THE HIGH SCHOOL YEARS

Moving to Garfield Park Housing Project
Attending high school; being in honors classes;
    tutoring athletes; participation in numerous
    extracurricular activities
Started working at community drug store as a
    waitress
My first boyfriends
Playing and fighting with my siblings
Visiting with cousins in Wisconsin
My first real job
My first real date with Melvin
Death of grandmother
Going on two proms
Graduating from high school
Going away to college

This was the *best* place we had ever lived. So much so, I thought that it was the best place in the world. It was called the Garfield Park Housing Projects. It was a newly constructed thirteen-story project building, with eleven apartments on each floor. A tall red brick and cement building with cement walls and cement floors, built especially for low-income residents. There were heat vents in every room, which meant that we didn't have to huddle around coal stoves and space heaters anymore for warmth. We had a nice, modern bathroom. There were no holes in the ceiling which meant that I didn't have to fear any rats looking down on me. No mice running around, at first. And we now had three bedrooms! At our last place, my sister and I slept in one small bedroom, Mama and 'that man' slept in the larger bedroom, and Robert and Reginald slept in the dining room which had been converted to a bedroom. Now my sister and I had our own bedroom, and Robert and Reginald had their own bedroom. And my mama and 'that man' had their own room.

There were plenty of picturesque flowers and thick, luscious green grass surrounding the thirteen-story building. It had a swimming pool, playground with monkey bars, swings and slides, and sitting areas which meant that we didn't have to play in the alleys anymore. Not one piece of broken glass was visible. And just as important, there was a laundry room on each floor, which meant no more lugging loads of laundry to the Laundromat. And all of it was so clean. It was a new building, and all of the families were so proud to have been selected to move in. The families had to apply for residency and undergo an interview and thorough home inspection to ensure that they met the city's sanitation requirements. We took ownership of our building, cleaning and mopping our porches every week. Each floor had a floor captain who made sure that the porches were cleaned and that everything was in order. Everything was so nice. There was a woman who would periodically come around to talk with my mother and stepfather to make sure that everything was all right and to conduct housekeeping inspections.

I was around lots of kids and made so many friends. I loved my neighbors on my floor. Most of the households were two-parent households with fathers who were gainfully employed. Of the ten other families on my floor, there lived a medical doctor, his wife, and their eight children; a school teacher and her husband who was a postman and their four children; some blue-collar workers; and just a couple of families headed by women. I enjoyed visiting the different families and playing with their children. In time, I even ventured to the other floors to visit the kids I had met in the playground and in the elevators.

**

Shortly after we moved in, I learned that Mama was pregnant again. This time she had a girl, April. By now, at the age of thirteen years old, I was beginning to have a better inkling of how babies were made. Not only did you have to be with a boy and raise your skirt, you also had to lay down in the same bed with him. That's how you get pregnant. I knew that because my girlfriends had told me so.

Whenever I would ask Mama about having babies, she would avoid the subject and ask me why I wanted to know.

"I just want to know," I would reply.

"Well, you're too young to know. Just keep your skirt down and your legs closed!"

Aha, I thought, *not only did you have to lie in a bed with a boy to get pregnant, and raise your skirt, you also have to have your legs open.*

I hated my new baby sister. She was fat, black, and ugly. My stepfather ooohed and ahhhed over her so much that it made me sick to my stomach. That baby cried all the time. And my stepfather would walk up and down the floor with her all night. Back and forth. Back and forth. Back and forth until April calmed down or went to sleep. Even after she was old enough to walk and talk, she would have those crying spells. And my stepfather would pick her up and walk that fifty-pound barracuda from one end of the apartment to another. And she had such disgusting, rotting baby teeth from eating all of the candy that 'that man' would give to her and his other kids. I hated her so much that I would often tease her and pinch her to make her cry and dared her to tell anyone about it.

About a year after April was born, Mama was pregnant again! *Dang*, I thought, *when is she going to stop having babies?* By that time, my stepfather had lost his job and would not even look for another one. Mama went to work as a domestic for the white folks to help make ends meet. She worked real hard, too hard, during that pregnancy, not only on her job but in the house, too. I remembered Mama, while pregnant, on her hands and knees waxing the floor with a rag. She wound up losing that baby. I was elated. *"I'm glad she lost that baby. I'm tired of having to take care of children. That would have been just one more baby for me to change his nasty diapers and wipe his snotty nose."*

But lo and behold! Another year, another baby. Mama was pregnant again! I was so embarrassed. Here I was, a sophomore, almost a junior in high school, and my mother was still having babies! My friends constantly teased me about it, saying that my mother was too old to still be having babies; that I should be the one having babies instead of her.

I really couldn't understand why my mother stayed with 'that man.' He was a horrible, horrible person. As time passed, I grew to downright hate him. Within a year after marrying my mother, he had returned to his old ways. He stopped attending church and became quite hostile whenever my mother would bring up the subject. He was an abusive alcoholic who would resort to violence as often as the sun shined and the moon beamed. He was mean to my mother, and they fought all of the time. Oh, the fights! There were so many of them! Every time he went out drinking at the bars, he would come back fighting at home. There were many nights that Robert, Berniece, and I would try to help our mother fight 'that man' back. I have vivid memories of all of us trying to protect her from him by hitting him with skillets, pots, and pans, yelling and crying, "Leave my mama alone! Leave my mama alone!" And Mama and we kids would fight him until he got tired or until Mama was able to break away and call the police. The police were not an uncommon sight at our house. Most times, they just took him away from the house for him to "cool off," never arresting him. Sometimes, he would return the same night, most times he would return the next day, apologizing to Mama, stating that he was sorry and would not beat her anymore. And Mama would always take him back.

And so, his joining the church meant absolutely nothing, just a ploy to get Mama to marry him or most likely the result of Mama's constant nagging to get married. His reversal to his old ways left a indelible impression on me. I learned, at a very early age, that you can't make someone change their ways. That no matter how you dressed it up, a snake was still a snake. No matter how much aluminum foil you covered it up with, shit was still shit and eventually would start smelling and stanking through that aluminum foil. *Lesson learnt—you can't change a person who does not want to change.*

***

He also showed favoritism with his children, often mistreating Mama's children of her first marriage (or what I thought to be Mama's first marriage—I learned many years later that Edna, Berniece, and Robert and I all had different fathers and only Edna was born within wedlock). He would bring home "goodies" for his children, calling them aside, taking them into his bedroom, closing the door behind him, and then handing out the goodies to them and admonishing them not to tell us. Berniece, Robert, and I were often left out of the "goody-sharing." But Reginald and April would always tell us about it and throw it up in our faces. "Ha, ha, ha, ha. We had some candy, and you didn't." He would give his kids quarters, nickels, and dimes and tell me, Berniece, and Robert that we couldn't even have a penny. This infuriated Mama. So much so that it caused other quarrels and fights. In the middle of the afternoon, in the early evening, and late at night.

"Your children ain't no better than these other children! Either all get something or all get nothing!"

I vividly remember one occasion in which Mama found 'that man' giving his kids some candy and not sharing it with us. Mama stormed into the bedroom and went on one of her all too common tirades. "Either all get something or none get anything!" That day Carl had a real big bag of mixed hard candies. Mama snatched the bag from his hand and flushed all of the candy down the toilet. Berniece, Robert, and I gasped! *What? What is she doing??? At least we could have had some of the candy! Now it's all gone. Down the toilet.* And so, at least that time, Mama was true to her word. Either all got some or nobody got any.

And he would slap us. And whip us. For the slightest little things. But not his kids. They were too good to be whipped. He would often coddle them and hug them and make them feel wanted. Berniece, Robert, and I felt like outcasts in our own home. We rarely got any type of affection, not from our stepfather (which I didn't want from him anyway) or from our mother, for Mama was not an affectionate person. To this day, none of us can remember Mama ever hugging or kissing us. All of us said that we could not ever remember Mama telling us that she loved us. Most of the time, she just fussed at us and made us do most of the household chores, for she was too tired from cleaning the white folks' houses all day and struggling to make ends meet. But I didn't know that. All I knew was that Mama was extremely strict and hard on me and that she never showed any affection toward me. And even if I did know that Mama was barely holding on to life, I wasn't sure that I could understand it.

Toward the latter term of Mama's last pregnancy, she and her husband got into a humongous fight. It was a knockdown, drag-out, no-holds-barred battle. Berniece, Robert, and I once again took out the skillets, pots, and pans (which we had never laid to rest for any length of time) to fight 'that man'. Even his oldest child, Reginald, joined in. For he was absolutely vicious that night. Hitting her in the face just like she was a man. Punching her in the stomach, didn't care that she was pregnant carrying his child. Stomping her. Swinging at the kids. Beating the living mess out of Mama until he got tired. After it was over, Mama called the police and had him arrested, and the police took him away, this time for good. He never returned to live with us again. Good, now Mama will stop having babies. Richard, the last of the children (thank God!), was born a couple of months after my stepfather left.

Many years later, my mother and I had a conversation about Carl's abusiveness. She asked me, "Do you remember when I used to sleep with the bedroom door closed? Do you know why I started sleeping with the door open? One night, Carl came home drunk and started choking me. I was laying down in the bed, with the bedroom door closed, and thought, *Oh, Lord, I'm being killed and none of my children can help me because they can't hear me.* That's when I started sleeping with the door open."

But I still could never understand why my mother stayed with that man. *Lesson learnt—sometimes it's beyond your ability to understand why some people stay in bad situations.*

***

About a year or so after my stepfather left for good, some white women started making periodic visits to our house. I never really paid any attention to them. They talked to my mother and sometimes made meaningless conversation with me. "Case workers," that's what they called them. But I wasn't a "case," so I had very little use for them or their conversations. I curtly answered what I considered to be stupid questions.

"How do you like school?"

Well, I was on the Honor Roll and a member of the National Honor Society, so, duh, what did they think? I vividly remember a conversation between the two case workers after they had questioned me about school.

In amazement, one said to the other, "That's a bastard child!"

Bastard child?? That was my first encounter with being ashamed of not having a father. In those days, being born out of wedlock was not accepted as it is today. It was a disgraceful sin not to have a father. "Bastard children" were frowned upon, often ostracized, and humiliated. Learning that I was a "bastard child" was devastating and, unknowingly, affected my self-image, pride, and psyche. But I comforted myself with the fact that no one, other than those case workers, knew about my birth status because we moved into the projects with a father. But it was a "dirty" little fact that I hid from others for just about all of my life.

For some reason, on these visits, they would go through our apartment, looking under the beds, and in the closets. *What are they looking for?* At other times, they would ask my mother where she got a particular item from, like the television or the radio. How nosy! *That's none of their business.* I resented their questions and the intrusion in our lives. But, after all, it had nothing to do with me, per se. That was my mother's business. At that time, I, poor thing, knew nothing about welfare, ADC (Aid to Dependent Children) and that those case workers were doing their job of making sure that a man was not living in the household and that my mother had no other source of income, no matter how meager it may be. Little did I know that in the future I would be truly embarrassed and humiliated, to the very depths of my soul, by those "case workers."

***

Occasionally, Mama worked as a domestic for the white folks, trying to make ends meet. After several years, she was able to secure a job working in the cafeteria at a neighborhood school, which enabled her to be home shortly after her kids got home. This job was especially beneficial for us because she was able to supplement her meager groceries with food smuggled from the school's cafeteria. We feasted on the leftovers and throwaway food from the cafeteria. The macaroni with beef and cheese, the peanut butter cookies, the hamburgers, and the fish fillets. Those foods were treats compared to the sandwiches we usually ate—banana and mayonnaise sandwiches, syrup sandwiches (Alaga syrup, that sweet, delicious dark cane syrup from the South, with yellow mustard), sugar and butter sandwiches and Spam sandwiches. And days-old donuts from the local bakery warmed up in the oven to remove the hardness and stale taste. But we loved those sandwiches and those stale donuts, especially the donuts because they were a real treat.

***

Although Mama did not show us affection, we did do a lot of family things together. Going to church, of course, which had basically become the center of our lives. Picnicking in the park with a portable grill and ice chest filled with food—sandwiches, fried chicken, and potato salad. Making homemade ice cream, cranking the handle over and over and over on the ice cream churn until the ice cream became solidified. So yummy, so mouthwatering, so scrumptious, so melt in your mouth delicious.

Mama was an avid baseball fan. But my siblings and I didn't really like going to the games because we didn't understand it. All we knew was that we were outside in the scorching hot sun watching some stupid men hitting and chasing a silly ball and that we couldn't afford to buy the fat, juicy, mouthwatering hot dogs sold in the park. We would actually drool over the hot dogs that we saw other people eating and enjoying. Mama would pack a small bag of popcorn, which we would nibble on during the game. And when we became thirsty, well that was just too bad, because Mama couldn't afford to buy the pop from the concession stand. And so, as much as Mama wanted her children to enjoy her favorite pastime, most of us developed a deep distaste for baseball, which lasted a lifetime.

***

At the beginning of one year, Mama bought us a duck for a pet. We named the duck "Quack! Quack!" You should have seen our happy faces, for we had never ever had a pet. (We didn't even know that it was quite unusual to have a duck for a pet.) That duck was treated better than the Queen of Sheba. We built a cage for it from a small crate we had scrounged from a local store, layering the bottom with newspapers and a pillow for the duck to sit on. We appropriated food from our mother's kitchen cabinets and refrigerator for its meals—oatmeal, lettuce and other vegetables, and scraps of meat from the dinner table. We also ensured that our duck had a bowl of fresh water every day.

Quack! Quack! really belonged to all of the kids on my floor. Because of housing regulations, no one could keep pets in their apartments. So, as Quack! Quack! grew bigger, in the summer of that year, Mama moved him, cage and all, to the laundry room on our floor. That's how the duck got to belong to everybody. Eagerly, each day, all of the kids would run home from school to the laundry room to feed and play with Quack! Quack!. We often took the duck out of the laundry room to chase it up and down the porch because it was comical to see how fast that duck could run, his body veering from side to side. Of course, poor Quack! Quack! didn't know what was going on. He was just running for his life.

One Sunday, about nine months after the duck became our pet, our mother did not accompany us to church but rather sent us on our way with an admonition to be good. When we returned from church, Mama had prepared a succulent meal. We had some kind of roasted meat drizzled in gravy, greens, cornbread, macaroni and cheese, and peach cobbler for dessert.

"Ooh, Mama, this is good!," we all kept exclaiming. "What is this meat? We never had this before. It's so tender and juicy! What is it?"

"It's your duck," Mama replied, looking evenly at us with unfeeling cold-blooded eyes.

"Yuk! No, Mama, you didn't!," we simultaneously said as we gagged on the duck, threw it up, and began to cry. How *could* she kill and cook our duck and then had the nerve to serve it to us? Our one and only pet that was so beloved! After I grew up, I wouldn't eat duck for many, many years. Well into my adult years. And for the longest, whenever I did, I thought of Quack! Quack! who was sacrificed to make a meal for us.

***

Some of my fondest memories were of visits to and from my cousins in Wisconsin. My mother and Uncle Robert had made a pact that their children would grow up knowing each other. They wanted their children to be close to each other to retain the tight-knit family unit that they had experienced in the South. All of their children were close in age to each other. During my junior high and high school years, each summer and on some holidays, Uncle Robert and his family would visit with Mama. And sometimes, Mama would take us to visit with Uncle Robert's family in Wisconsin. These visits would range from a few days to a month.

Uncle Robert, a deacon in his church, was a kindly man, who looked very much like my grandfather. Tall and dark-skinned, he was a good-natured friendly man who spoke in soft tones. He was married to a woman named Miss Natasha, who was mean and seemed to be evil-spirited. I was scared of her and did my best to please her. But mostly, I just stayed out of her way. But I loved my uncle, almost as much as my godfather and Uncle Harry.

I especially liked going to Wisconsin because of the mouth-watering meals that Miss Natasha would prepare. She would create meals with several types of meats. That never happened at my house—we always had only one meat, if that, for our meals. And Miss Natasha could cook a mean mouthwatering pound cake and succulent blueberry pie! Their meals were on a different cycle than I was used to. They had their heavy meal, dinner around 4:00 pm and a lighter meal which they called supper, around 7:00 pm.

I loved my five cousins, especially Leonard and Yvette. I liked the other ones, too, but Leonard and Yvette were my favorites. Oh, we thoroughly enjoyed each other! Playing games with one another and other neighborhood kids, going to the park, and playing in the playground.

I secretly had a crush on Leonard, who was a couple of years older than me. He, too, was tall and dark-skinned with a deep voice for his age. I knew that he could never be my boyfriend because he was my cousin, but that didn't stop me from occasionally thinking about it. And I thought that Leonard had a secret crush on me because of the way he would sometimes look at me. But both of us knew the rules of taboo and kept our emotional and physical distance from one another.

There was something so sexually attractive to me about Yvette and I felt that she was sexually attracted to me. She had full plump lips, and her breasts were more fully developed than mine, which was no great feat for my breasts were still developing. And being the young girls that we were, with actively developing hormones, we began exploring each other's bodies. We knew not to mess with "dem boys," but nobody said anything about messing with girls. We weren't lesbians or bisexual, we were just curious. In the summer of my freshman year in high school, Uncle Robert brought his family to spend the week with us. That summer, Yvette and I began exploring each other's bodies. It was not too hard to do because Yvette shared the bedroom with Berniece and me (Yvette and I slept in my bed), while April slept in the room with Mama. It all started innocently enough. On a few occasions at night, when everyone was asleep, or so we thought, lying in bed with each other with our hormones beginning to flow, it all became sort of natural. It began one night with the touching, exploring one another's bodies. Real pleasure came from rubbing on Yvette's body and kissing her full lips. Experiencing the sensation of caressing and kissing her rounded breasts, getting sexually aroused, rubbing our little pussies until discharge flowed out. It felt so good! We only did it for a few times over the course of that summer visit, and then, having savored the ecstasy of sexual satiation and also feeling that we may be doing something wrong, something bad, we stopped. There was no more need for it. And we never, ever spoke about it to each other. Never, ever. Even when we were doing it. Even after we stopped doing it. Perhaps it was a sense of remorse. Perhaps it was a sense of guilt. I don't know. That chapter of our lives was closed. *Lesson learnt—curiosity is an inquisitive creature that can lead you to places that you would otherwise never explore.*

***

Mama would take us to church conferences and workshops, and sometimes we would return to the South to visit relatives. I especially remembered the train rides back and forth. I couldn't understand why we always had to debark in Nashville and board the back cars of the train. Only the Black folks had to do that. *Why do we have to change cars, Mama?* I had no inkling about Jim Crow. Other times, we took the Greyhound bus Down South. Mama would pack shoeboxes filled with crispy fried chicken, various fruits, and mouthwatering slices of pound cake for us to consume during the long ride. I always thought that my mother prepared those shoebox lunches for convenience and to save money. My young mind still did not know about that strange man named Jim Crow who would not allow us to eat in the same restaurants as white folks. On one occasion, we had enough money to purchase a meal at one of the stops along the way. When my sister and I went into the restaurant, we were instructed by the wait staff to go around to the back and weren't allowed to eat our food inside the restaurant.

"Why, Mama, why can't we eat inside?"

"Hush, child," Mama replied.

At the many stops along the bus route after we passed the Mason-Dixon Line (which I knew absolutely nothing about), there were signs posted on the water fountains and bathrooms, *For Colored Only* and *For Whites Only*. Mama instructed us about which ones to use.

"Why do we have separate water fountains and bathrooms? We don't have those at home."

"You ask too many questions. Just do as I tell you."

I loved our brief but infrequent excursions to the South. I got a chance to play with my girlfriend, Patricia, and my cousins, as well as to visit my godparents and grandparents. But, to my regret, we always had to return back Up North, to our other life, with its own peculiar problems for me.

***

Although I tried my best to please her, my mother and I were never close. And, as I grew older, we grew apart even more. I had a tendency to talk back to my mother (and others), to challenge and question decisions, earning me the reputation of being a "smart mouth." Mama was always nagging and complaining. Outside of schoolwork and church, I could never please my mother. The house wasn't clean enough. Why didn't I wash all of the clothes? Why are there dirty dishes in the sink? Why didn't you help the kids with their homework? (*Dang, I didn't ask you to have all these kids. Why I gotta take care of them? They ain't my responsibility.*) Mama always wanted to dominate me in everything. She constantly expressed a distrust of me. "Are you messing around with 'dem boys'?" "You'd better not call yourself trying to have a boyfriend." "Why was that boy talking to you?" She was extremely strict in my upbringing. Mama would even check my dirty panties in the dirty clothes laundry basket looking for some evidence that I was sexually active. Even though she was proud of my academic achievements, and would often boast of them, she never allowed herself to become close to me. And even if she had tried, I would have rejected her advances because that woman got on my last nerve.

When Mama was really mad at me, she would call me a heifer. Back then, being called a heifer was almost the equivalent of being called a bitch, only much worse because of the way it was said with such vengeance. The words would spitefully roll off her tongue in an amplified voice. "*You, heifer, you!*" drawing out and almost shouting the word "heifer."

Another one of Mama's favorite biting critical descriptions of me was to call me an African. "*You African, you!*" Oh, Lord! Being called an African was worse than being called a heifer. Back then, there was no Black pride movement. And everything we had heard and seen on TV about Africans conjured up images of wild, wide-eyed, pitch-black, almost-naked natives running around with spears in their hands, speaking in unintelligible tongues, and eating white men from a cauldron of boiling water. So, to be called an African was the utmost of insults.

Mama also warned us not to drink coffee. "Coffee will make you black," she said whenever one of us asked to taste her coffee, which she drank each morning. And, of course, no one ever wanted to be black. I figured that that admonishment applied only to growing children because Mama drank coffee every morning and she wasn't black.

One piece of priceless advice (or so she thought) that she gave to me about marriage was to not marry a dark-skinned man. "If you do," she warned, "your children will turn out black." *And who wanted black-skinned children? Lesson learnt—being black is undesirable.*

***

Because I was the oldest, I was often stuck with taking care of my younger brothers and sisters, which caused a lot of resentment on my part, especially when I wanted to be with my friends. I had learned my childhood lessons of motherhood preparation well. By the age of thirteen, I could cook a mean meal: fried chicken, macaroni and cheese, sweet potatoes, green vegetables, and corn bread. I knew how to do the laundry, clean the house, and sew. In effect, I was my younger siblings' surrogate mother. I was responsible for them from the time I got out of school until my mother arrived home, when she went to church and sometimes after that.

To Mama's credit, she also taught the boys how to sew, iron, and cook. She taught the girls not only how to cook and clean house but also how to make minor household repairs and how to splice the wires in appliances to make them work again. She admonished the girls to never have to depend upon a man and admonished the boys to never have to depend upon a woman. *Lesson learnt—don't depend on anyone else; learn to do for yourself*

***

Berniece, Robert, and I frequently quarreled and fought. When we were not fighting each other, Berniece and I would team up against our oldest brother, Robert, who was younger than both of us, but he was real big and tall for his age. Even at the age of ten, he had to carry ID with him so that he could pay the children's fare on the bus. So it took the both of us to win a fight against him. One day, we started ganging up on Robert, team-tagging our vicious hits and kicks against him, but it was a losing battle for both of us. So Berniece ran outside of the apartment with Robert running after her. Berniece made a quick U-turn back into the apartment, and I quickly locked the door behind her.

"Ha, ha! We got you," we gleefully yelled out from behind the locked door.

Robert was angrier than a raging bull because we had gotten the best of him. He wanted to kick our asses. He banged and banged on the door.

"Let me in!"

"Is you crazy?", we yelled at him. Safe and secure, because we knew that Robert couldn't get back into the house and that our mother would be coming home soon, we began watching television. About five minutes later, we looked out and saw Robert removing the screen from the window.

"Oh, no! We're in trouble now!" For, even together, we couldn't control Robert when he was that angry. We hurriedly checked to make sure that the window was locked. Good! He can't get in. But, somehow, Robert started prying that window loose. We watched in sheer dread and fear as Robert worked the window loose, with murder in his heart and eyes. *What are we going to do?* All we could think of was to run into our bedroom and barricade the door with the dresser so that Robert couldn't kill us. And that's what we did. Robert finally got in through that window and headed for our room. He tried to force the door open by pressing his big oversized body against it. With all our might, Berniece and I kept pushing the dresser, straining ourselves, against the door in an effort to keep him out. We were terribly afraid for we knew that Robert was really going to hurt us, real bad. Possibly kill us. As he was shoving through the door, almost in, Mama came home. Just in the nick of time to save us from being mauled to death by him.

"Robert, what are you doing?," Mama yelled. When we heard Mama's voice, we were exceedingly relieved.

"Mama! Mama! Guess what Robert did?," we exclaimed.

When Mama heard that Robert torn the screen down and broke through that window, guess what? She beat the hell out of him. Which made Berniece and me real happy!

"You shouldn't have been messing with us," we taunted, as Robert was getting his ass whipped, even though we were the ones who started the fight.

Another time, we convinced Robert to play a game of cowboys and Indians with us. We explained the game to him. He was the cowboy, the good guy. We were the bad guys, the Indians. We were going to tie him up and do war dances around him, making Indian warlike noises. And when it was his turn, he could do the same, pretending to shoot us. So Robert agreed. We then tied Robert up to a chair with a rope and made sure the rope was tied really tightly. But we had no intention of doing a war dance. Instead, we pranced around him like in musical chairs. And each time one of us flounced around Robert's face, we would hit him in the chest and slap him on his face. Poor Robert! There was nothing he could do about it. He couldn't get loose because we had made sure that the rope was tightly tied around him. We beat him until we got good and tired. And all poor Robert could do was sit there and take it, resigned to his fate, but determined to get his revenge on us one day.

***

But I really detested Berniece 'cause she was Miss Goody Two-Shoes. Always sucking up to our mother. And I disliked Robert 'cause he was bad. Always getting into trouble. Stealing. Stealing Berniece's and my hard-earned babysitting and errand-running money which we thought we had carefully hidden from him. No matter where we hid our piggy banks, Robert would always find them. And then to hear him brag about it. "Yeah, you thought you could hide your money. But I found it and spent it." Lying. Always lying. Trying to get Berniece and me on Mama's bad side. Making up stories about us. Bad-mouthing the teachers. Ditching school. Always instigating fights. That's why Berniece and I banded together against him—for mutual protection.

And I didn't like the baby girl, April, either because she was fat, ugly, and spoiled rotten. And I had no particular feelings about Reginald and Richard, the last baby. *Lesson learnt—just because you're born into it doesn't mean that you like your family, but there's nothing you can do about it. Make the best of it.*

***

Yet, I had some fond memories of my life in the projects. And some experiences that I would never forget. Robert was forever getting into trouble. He just had a penchant for it. About a year after we moved in, he made the bad mistake of crossing Mickey, one of the neighborhood's gang leaders. I wasn't sure whether he had crossed Mickey or if Mickey, for no reason, decided to just pick on him. Just like, for no reason, I had picked on Sharon. Almost every day, Mickey would pick on Robert. Hitting him, calling him names, teasing him, and daring him to hit him back. Ordinarily, because of his gigantic stature for his age, Robert would have taken up the challenge. But Mickey was the neighborhood gang leader. And all the kids respected him. Actually, we feared him. He was taller than most of us, fair-skinned with wavy hair, and a mean sneer permanently etched on his face. Mickey would knock the little kids down for no reason at all, just to show his toughness and King of the Mountain attitude, and no one would challenge him. In fact, whether out of deference or out of fear, most of us would hurriedly vacate the playground when he and his boys showed up.

Several times each week, Robert would come home upset and crying because Mickey had been picking on him. I got fed up with Mickey and wished that he would pick on somebody his own age and size. I, too, was scared of Mickey but was quite outraged that he had selected my brother to be his whipping boy. Even though Robert was bad and I didn't particularly like him, he was still my brother.

One day, before 'that man' left for good, all the children were in the playground playing as usual. Swinging on the swings. Climbing through the monkey bars. Playing on the jungle gym. Jumping rope, and playing hopscotch. Mickey and his boys walked in. He walked straight up to Robert and started hitting him. Upon seeing that once again Mickey was picking on Robert, I became greatly enraged.

"Leave my brother alone. Go pick on someone your own size," I screamed.

"And if I don't, what you going to do about it?"

"I'm going to beat you up," I replied.

It took a lot of courage to stand up to Mickey. I was only 5'4" weighing 89 pounds, standing up to his 5'8", 160 lb frame. But I was absolutely furious. I was tired of this shit, just like Sharon was tired of my shit. All I could see was red. I had no fear. As was his habit, Mickey went directly over and hit my brother again. You could see the terror and pain in Robert's eyes. I couldn't take it anymore. I went to Mickey and furiously started hitting him. A crowd of kids began gathering around.

"Get him! Show him!"

I went wild. I was hitting him. Stretching my small arms trying to strike him in the face. I was scratching him. On his arms, on his hands. Punching him in his stomach. I was beating Mickey's butt! All the time yelling, "I'm tired of you messing with my brother. Leave him alone!" And, for a minute, I appeared to be winning the fight. Mickey was blocking my punches and wasn't hitting me back. Then, he coolly bent down and snatched both of my legs from under me. I hit the cement ground with a loud thud, promptly knocking me unconscious. He stood triumphantly over me, grinning. The crowd was silenced, stunned with disbelief that Mickey used such an underhanded technique on a girl nearly half his size. They just stood around staring at him and at me lying on the ground.

"Dawg, he knocked her out! Naw, she dead! She ain't movin."

"She dead!"

Robert ran upstairs to tell Mama what had happened. Within a few minutes, my stepfather came down and saw me lying on the ground unconscious.

"Leave my daughter alone," he yelled.

"Whatya gonna do about it, old man?" Mickey challengingly asked.

My stepfather shoved Mickey aside, picked me up like a limp rag doll, threw me over his shoulder, and took me to our apartment. That was the only time I didn't mind having my stepfather hold me in his arms because I felt protected from Mickey. That fight was the talk of the hood for many weeks. And, after that, Mickey stopped messing with my brother, which taught me another lesson, the lesson that Sharon had learned many years before. *Lesson learnt—no matter if you do get your ass beat, don't let nobody walk all over you.*

***

During my early teenage years, I became the "family babysitter." I often babysat for my older sister, Edna. By this time, she had four children. And I would often spend whole weekends with her. Cleaning the house, doing the laundry, bathing the kids, going to the grocery store. Edna was calling on me more often to come and babysit on the weekends. Oftentimes, Edna was home while I was babysitting. I enjoyed those times with Edna. I didn't mind watching my nieces and nephew, who were born around the same time as my youngest sisters and brothers. I would help Edna clean the house, cook breakfast and dinner, and watch after the kids. I even got paid. And the best part of it all was that I was away from my mother's constant nagging and complaining.

Years later, Edna told me that the reason she had me over to her house so often was because she was severely depressed and I was her lifeline. Unbeknownst to anyone, her husband regularly abused her, both physically and emotionally. Edna said that she was going to counseling at the time. She said that when I was around her, she was able to hold onto the precious little bit of sanity that she had.

***

Around the age of fourteen, I also began babysitting and cleaning house for Uncle Harry. He was a school teacher and had a school teacher wife. (He had earned a permanent place of love and respect in my heart as my most favorite uncle because he had taken me to Mrs. Little Jack's for my eighth grade graduation.) They lived on the south side and were considered "well-to-do." I didn't care too much for his wife because she was uppity and such a stickler about cleaning. She would even do the white glove test on the furniture that I dusted and on the back and bottom of the toilet bowl and base which I had meticulously cleaned.

By the time I was sixteen, I had changed so many diapers and fed so many mouths that I resolved to never have a child. *Who wants to be responsible for wiping snotty noses and changing shitty diapers all of their life?*

But I loved my uncle. He reminded me so much of my god-father and Uncle Jimmy, tall and gentle and soft spoken. I spent many weekends at his house babysitting and cleaning. I really didn't mind because they would give me money for the chores I performed. And it wasn't like I was missing out on any dates because my mother wouldn't let me date anyway, saying that I was too young. Furthermore, the babysitting and cleaning jobs gave me the opportunity to be out of the house away from Mama.

Uncle Harry was also an investment broker. He started Mama and our family on our way to accumulating wealth by starting an investment plan for us. All Mama had to pay was $25 a month, and we would be on our way to riches. In fact, he even contributed the first payment. But after only a few months, Mama stopped contributing and cashed in that little bit. Even $25 a month was too much for her.

***

I never had any concept of money or money matters. Mama would complain, after I started working, that money ran through my hands like water. I knew that my family didn't have as much money as other families. Then again, I knew families that had the same amount or less than ours. Mama would tell me that times were bad, but that didn't mean anything to me. I was in my own fantasy world of wealth and riches, for I was determined to be rich or, at the very least, quite comfortable.

In fact, I didn't even know that we were "poor." I often carried my lunch to school or would go home for lunch. But, then again, so did a lot of the kids. I lived only five minutes from the school. I liked going home for lunch because it gave me the opportunity to play around with the other kids. Sometimes, the boys that I was trying to "talk to" or even "talking to" as the required preliminary step for "going together" would walk me back and forth from lunch. And sometimes we would even sneak a quick furtive kiss in the stairwell.

At times, Mama would make homemade bread, telling us that it was much healthier than store-bought white bread. "Fresh out of the oven," she would proudly say. Then she would cut the loaf of bread into real thick slices and would make our lunch sandwiches with those horrendously thick slices of bread. Whenever I took those sandwiches for lunch the other kids would make fun of me and mercilessly tease me, often playing the dozens on me. *"Oh, yo' mama too po' to buy white bread!"* I was so embarrassed. But I would eat those sandwiches anyway because I was hungry and didn't have any money to buy one of those juicy hamburger lunches and the delectable, lip-smacking peanut butter cookies. I only had enough money to buy the white milk, which costs three cents. Most times I couldn't buy the chocolate milk because it costs five cents. But I still never considered myself poor. We just didn't have enough money, that's all. Just like a lot of many kids in school.

Other times, Mama made meatless meals. Those were a treat for me and my siblings. My favorite was peaches and dumplings. Those thick slices of peaches, cooked in heavy, sweet, cinnamony, and nutmeg syrup loaded with dumplings. All of us waited in anticipation for the dumplings to finish cooking as we smelled the sweet aroma of the peaches and cinnamon and nutmeg drifting through the apartment. It was so deliciously good! I didn't know that my mother only made that dish when she couldn't afford to buy meat for our meals.

The advent of food stamps was my wake up call to the fact that we were truly poor. When food stamps first came out, everybody knew that they were for the poor folks. They didn't use real money to pay for food items, so you couldn't hide the fact that you were using food stamps. I, along with some of my friends, would make derisive statements about poor people who had to use food stamps. Then, when I was sixteen years old, my very own special moment of reckoning came. I had somehow suspected that we were poor, but I really didn't know it. Not until my special day of reckoning.

"Mai, go to the corner store and get me a loaf of bread and a package of bologna."

"Okay, Mama, where's the money?"

"Here," and handed me a booklet of those ugly green and brown food stamps.

"Food Stamps! When did we get these? I can't go to the store and use these food stamps! I'm too embarrassed!"

"Embarrassed or not, you're going and you're going to use these food stamps."

"Mama, please don't make me go. Please!"

And, I, realizing that my mother was not going to change her mind, promptly broke down and cried, tears flowing down my face.

"Food stamps mean that you're poor."

"Well, child. We are. We are poor."

Reluctantly, and with tears still filling my eyes, I slowly walked to the corner store. Upon entering, I saw a couple of my friends. I was petrified. *I can't let them see me using these stamps. They'll know that I'm poor.* And poor was the last thing that I wanted to be. After briefly greeting my friends, I slinked around the store, pretending to examine different items for cost and content. Reading the nutritional content of cereals, canned goods, anything with writing on it. Even though I didn't understand any of the nutritional labels, I knew that I had to pass time until my friends left the store. After walking around that small store for what seemed like ten minutes and making sure that my friends had left, I hurriedly purchased the white bread and bologna, refusing to make eye contact with the store clerk who knew, by the method in which I paid for the food, that I, too, was poor.

Just like all those other poor Black people that came into his filthy, smelly store. I could feel his disdain for me gushing through him as I paid for my purchase with the food stamps. I could actually feel his sneering eyes looking at me with such contempt. What a traumatic moment for me! I returned home, with my head held down and my spirit broken. Never did I imagine that later in life that I'd be glad to get a hold of some food stamps.

***

Under my mother's strict rules and observant eyes, I grew up living a very sheltered existence. I wasn't allowed to wear makeup. My mother said that I had to be sixteen before I could wear lipstick. *All the other girls are wearing lipstick*, I vainly protested. But, with my girlfriends' help, I was beginning to learn how to be slick and how to circumvent my mother's numerous restrictions. My friends let me use their makeup and taught me how to apply it after I left for school in the mornings and how to take it off before I returned home in the afternoons.

I couldn't date when my friends started dating. My girlfriends started dating when they were thirteen years old. But me! I had to wait until I was sixteen. *Sixteen must be a magical age*, I thought.

And I'd better not even think of cursing. If I said the words "liar," "lie," or even "fool," I was instantly slapped on my mouth by my mother. I couldn't question my mother about anything. Being a naturally curious child, I was fond of asking why this or why that. To which my mother would respond, *Because I said so.* Never explaining anything.

Oftentimes, I would ask her questions about the Bible and God. After all, I was virtually a child of the church. I would ask why Jesus did this or that, why God ordered his servants to kill people, and why did we have to go to church all of the time. My mother's usual answer was that it was in the Bible, and that was that. When I would continue to press on with more questions, she would exasperatedly say, *Because God said so!* When she said that, I knew that I would be getting no further answers from her and that the conversation was over. Which really pissed me off and made me more determined to find out why things were as they were, not just because my mother or God said so. And so, at least once or twice each week, I was slapped on my mouth for asking "why." *Smart-mouthed*, my mother called me.

***

When I turned thirteen my mother pulled me aside and told me that she wanted to talk to me about "the facts of life"—becoming a woman. I curtly ended that conversation because I knew that my mother was talking about me starting my period. This was the first time that my mother had tried to talk to me about anything personal. But it was too late. The girls in my gym class had already told me about that, and, as far as I was concerned, they knew more than my mother. The girls also talked about boyfriends, sex, and having babies. From them I learned that I was wrong about how babies are conceived. You had to do more than just lie down with a man with your skirt up and your legs open. You had to *do it*. I hadn't the slightest ideas about what *doing it* meant. But I didn't let them know that. I pretended to be as knowledgeable as they appeared to be.

My first period, at the age of thirteen, about a month after my mother tried to have her woman-to-woman talk with me, was memorable for it marked a milestone in my life. Never mind that I didn't have another one until almost a year later. I was on my way to becoming a woman. What I didn't know about menstrual cycles, I quickly found out. The cramps. And washing those nasty period rags. For the most part, we couldn't afford to buy sanitary napkins and had to use rags made from old diapers. Tampons had not yet been invented, and, even if they had been, my mother would not have been able to afford them. My mother taught me how to threefold the rags just right to fit inside my panties and to secure them with safety pins. The rags between my skinny legs made me so uncomfortable. I caught the dickens learning how to walk with those rags between my legs without walking gap-legged. Sometimes the blood ran through the rags and soiled my skirt when I was in school. I would try to cover it up and run home to change. I dreaded washing those rags. The blood. The reddish-brown blood clots. The smell. How disgusting! But faithfully, I would wash them when they became soiled, hanging them up to dry in the bathroom for the next use. Embarrassed and fumbling for words when Robert asked what those rags were for. But there was one good side to being on your period, I discovered. When you were on your period, you got excused from gym. And so, sometimes, even when I wasn't, I was on my period. *Lesson learnt— sometimes bad things can work on your behalf.*

***

My mother did let me start wearing stockings when I turned thirteen. At least that was something. My aunt Mamie called herself trying to help me in my quest to achieve womanhood by providing stockings for me to wear. The stockings were a horrible, bright reddish-brown color. Red fox is what they called them. Those reddish-brown stockings on my dark brown legs made quite a sight and was a source of humiliation for me, for everyone knew that they were the cheapest stockings you could buy. But I couldn't do any better. My mother was grateful that Mamie was supplying the stockings. And Mamie was glad to put her two cents in about what I should be wearing. And I resolved that when I was old enough to get a job, I would get some brown-colored stockings that matched my skin tone. But I couldn't get a job until I turned sixteen. Back then, children were not allowed to work until they turned sixteen because they didn't have those so-called poverty programs that allowed children fourteen years and older to work after school. "Just wait until I start working," I would often muse, "I'll have everything and do everything I want." Or so I thought.

***

Life at home gradually became intolerable for me. My mother was a devout believer and disciple of corporal punishment. She was a fervent disciplinarian who strongly believed in the Christian biblical teaching of "spare the rod, spoil the child." Poor me and my siblings. All our lives we received beatings and old-fashioned, down-home "whuppings." With a belt. With the ironing cord. With an extension cord. With a broom. With the mop. With whatever Mama and 'that man' could put their hands on. We received whippings for any and all infractions, real or imagined, by our mother. From the time that I was eleven (upon my return from the South) until the time that I was seventeen, I constantly received whippings and mouth and facial blows from my mother. My grandparents and godparents had never laid a hand on me, much less whip me. *Spare the rod and spoil the child.* I certainly wasn't spoiled. My mother would whip most of her kids mercilessly (except the younger ones) in addition to the slaps on the mouth that I received. The turning point in the whippings came when I was almost seventeen years old. That was the last time Mama slapped me, and it was for being "smart-mouthed."

Mama had begun yet another one of her tirades about how much she had sacrificed for her children. *I did this and I did that. Ad infinitum.* Like trying to put us on a guilt trip. That we should be appreciative of all that she had done for us. I hadn't asked Mama to have all of those kids. Each of the older children had different fathers (Edna, me, Berniece, and Robert), and I felt that since Mama had them, she should provide for them. That was her decision to have those children.

I was so fed up with hearing how much she had sacrificed for us (I heard that speech at least once a month), that I responded with *I didn't ask to be born.*

"What did you say?," Mama asked scathingly.

"I didn't ask to be born," I repeated with a roaring rage in my voice.

Mama promptly slapped me hard on my face. After Mama slapped me, I told her that she'd better not *ever* do that again.

"And what are you going to do about it?," she demanded.

"I'll slap you back," I angrily and viciously replied, with anger and murder in my heart and voice and eyes. And I meant every word of it. To her credit and good sense, she never hit me again. I guess she had learned the lesson of *when someone tells you that they're tired of you messing with them, you'd better believe it!*

***

Long after we were grown my siblings and I were fond of saying that we would still be visiting our mother in prison if the current child abuse laws were on the books when we were growing up. Sometimes we would reminisce about the whippings we took when we were children and would show off our permanent scars left by the beatings. And none of us could remember our mother ever kissing or hugging us. In a later conversation with me, Berniece recalled the situation in which I threatened to hit our mother back.

Berniece said that if I had hit her back, she would have jumped on me. (*Well, she would have just had her ass beat, too.*) I accused Berniece of being a goody two-shoes.

Berniece explained, "You didn't understand. I believed Mama when she said that she brought us in this world and she could take us out of it. Your problem was that you didn't believe it. And that's why you had so many problems."

***

Mama was the main disciplinarian, although our stepfather would join in sometimes when Mama was whipping Robert. Watching them whip Robert was like watching the pagans throw the Christians to the lions. The whippings were brutal and vicious. Mama said that she was trying to whip the devil out of Robert. It didn't work because he kept being bad and doing bad things. One day, she found out that he had touched a girl. I couldn't understand what was so bad about touching a girl. After all, in some fashion or other, he touched us every day and we were girls. But he must have touched this girl in the wrong spot because Mama was *mad*. She began whipping Robert with a livid, hellfire, and brimstone vengeance.

Robert only made it worse by running. That was one thing that all of us learned at a very early age. A whipping is made worse by running from it. It seemed as if the chase boosted Mama's adrenaline, giving her more energy to beat "the living hell" out of us. When it came time for the whipping for touching the girl, Robert ran and Mama couldn't catch him. Her old, mean, hateful husband joined in the chase, with a look of sheer pleasure in his eyes at the anticipation of whipping one of Mama's kids with her total consent and active participation.

With both of them chasing him around the house, Robert looked like a wild, wounded animal desperately trying to free himself from a trap. Finally, he ducked under his bed and, momentarily, felt safe.

"They can't whip me under the bed," Robert reasoned.

Mama bent down and thrust the belt under the bed trying to make contact with Robert's skin. But Robert rolled over out of her reach. Mama's husband tried to do the same, but to no avail. Then her husband had a real bright idea. He closed the bedroom door, but I cracked the door open so that I could see what was going on. 'That man' pulled the mattress and box spring off the bed. They could see Robert lying on the floor under the bed frame. Robert was now truly trapped. 'That man,' with malice in his heart and a depraved look in his evil eyes, smirked with glee and anticipation, very much the same as a hunter does when closing in on his prey. Then he pulled up the bed frame, exposing Robert in all his frailty. And they proceeded to whip the living hell out of him, with a belt and an extension cord, each taking a turn at administering painful lashes to his body. Robert hollered and screamed uncontrollably and thrashed around futilely, unable to avoid the instruments of chastisement. It was truly a terrifying, heart-wrenching sight. I was agonized by the sight of it all, and with tears in my eyes cried out, *Stop whipping him! Stop whipping him! Whip me instead*, which, of course they did not do but continued to viciously whip Robert until they tired of the sport. Robert later said that that beating almost turned him into a homosexual—he vowed never to touch another girl again. A vow, which of course, he broke.

***

We never forgot those whippings. I remember one time when Mama said that she was going to whip me. I forget what it was for, probably for being smart-mouthed. But she was too tired to whip me that day because she had had a hard day at work. So, she told me that she would whip me later. The rest of the evening passed and Mama didn't whip me. The next day passed and Mama didn't whip me. Another day passed and she didn't whip me. *Oh good*, I thought, *she's forgotten about it.*

On the third day when I got home from school, Mama called me into her bedroom and calmly said, "Mai, do you remember that whipping I promised you? Well, it's time," and proceeded to whip "the hell" out of me.

On another occasion, Mama caught Robert and tied him up in a sheet and slung him over the corner of a door, which was quite a feat, considering Robert's size. Then she proceeded to beat him through the sheet with a broom.

Whenever she would whip us, she would say that she was doing it because she loved us. *This is love??? Hate me!* I resolved that if, by any chance, I ever had children, I would never subject them to the abuse Mama did to us. And the killing part about it was that, in later years, Mama felt justified about all of those beatings. "Well, I must have known what I was doing. Y'all turned out alright." Which, in my estimation, was in spite of, not because of. And we didn't all turn out alright, especially Edna, me, and Robert. We were, if truth be told, emotionally fucked up. And Robert really had a fucked up life.

***

I looked forward to attending school every day. School was my escape from my family and the responsibilities there. School was a place where I could have fun as well as learn. I eagerly looked forward to walking to and from school with my friends, eating lunch with them, and clowning around with them during school. I couldn't hang with them after school because I had to go straight home. Another one of my mother's rules. This was a rule I couldn't break because my mother's job at a nearby school allowed her to arrive home around the same time as me and the other kids.

Because I was a clown, I tended to have a lot of friends. They weren't real friends, in the true sense of the word. But I didn't know that. For at that tender age, I didn't know the meaning of a true friend. I thought that anyone who talked and smiled at you, laughed at your jokes, and sometimes hung out with you was a friend. So, according to my limited and yet broad definition, I had plenty of friends. As my life progressed, I would learn the hard way about the true meaning of "friend." *Lesson learnt—a friend can be your worst enemy.*

***

I was also quite bright. Almost gifted. Although I tended to play down that part. This was especially true in high school. Most of my schoolmates did not value education. Smart kids were outcasts, nerds. The last thing I wanted to be labeled as was a nerd. I wanted to be Popular, to be one of the "in-crowd." The in-crowd consisted of the good dressers, the cheerleaders, the ones who could hang out, and those "fast girls" and "mannish boys," the girls who were near white with good hair and thin lips, and the athletes (most of whom were dumb, but Popular).

I wasn't particularly good-looking. In fact, by some standards, I was downright ugly. I had to wear "coke-bottle" eyeglasses, as plastic lenses had not yet been invented. I had a pug nose and big lips. And was dark-skinned. Not good by the in-crowd's standards. And I had a gold bridge on my front teeth, the result of a dentist yanking out the front tooth, instead of filling the cavity. That's what they did with their poor clients. Just yank out the tooth, insert an ugly false tooth, and put in a gold bridge. At the time that it happened, it was okay, even almost cool, 'cause there were so many Black folks walking around with gold bridges and gold teeth. However, years later, when it was no longer in vogue, that gold bridge was a constant source of embarrassment for me. But there was nothing I could do about it.

To look like one of the in-crowd girls, I tried sleeping with a clothespin on my nose to make it aquiline and on my lips to make them thin. I rubbed Nadinola on my face every night to lighten up my skin tone. After regular usage, I looked quite strange because I didn't know that I should have also applied the Nadinola to my neck as well. So, for a while, I was two-toned, with my neck being noticeably darker than my face.

***

At age sixteen, I finally turned old enough to start wearing a light coat of make-up, with my mother's approval (although I had been sneaking it on for a couple of years). However, I never wore red lipstick. That was a no-no. Red was the devil's color, sinful, according to my mother. I remembered my grandfather saying that red lips on a dark-skinned woman made her lips look like a horse's ass. I tried to make my lips look smaller by applying lipstick just beneath the top and just above the bottom lips to give them the illusion of being smaller.

I tried to fit in with the in-crowd as best as I could, but I could never fully do so. The Popular girls would sometimes sneer at me and make disparaging remarks about my efforts to "fit in," like "You're too dark to try out for the cheerleading team" and "Yeah, you may be smart, but you won't fit in with our social club." And so, despite my best efforts, I was never fully accepted by the in-crowd. *Lesson learnt—try to live up to your own expectations and no one else's.*

***

During the course of high school, I did have a couple of boyfriends, and, periodically, my mother would let me attend the high school dances. The first high school dance that I attended was permanently etched in my mind. It was something that I would *never ever* forget because I had been s-o-o-o humiliated.

Through flirtation and just out-and-out asking, I managed to get Arthur to take me to the freshman dance. Arthur lived in my building and was a year ahead of me in school. His sisters and I would often play and talk together and visit one another. Arthur was a catch. He was a nerd, but he was a good-looking nerd. And quite a good catch. I had had a crush on him since I was in elementary school in the old neighborhood. Arthur had to ask my mother's permission to take me to the dance. But that wasn't the bad part. The bad part was that my mother escorted us to the freshman dance. She walked the three blocks to the school with us. None of the other kids had their parents escort them to the freshman dance. That was humiliating enough. But it got worse. When the dance was over, my mother was standing right there outside the school's front door, waiting to walk us home! How could a girl be grown when her mother was walking with her and her date to and from dances? It gave me another reason to dislike her.

***

My role as a clown immensely helped me in being somewhat accepted by the in-crowd. I was always able to make others laugh and was often the brunt of cruel jokes. But I didn't mind because the elite crowd was paying me some attention. And I considered them to be my friends because they were friendly. When they weren't being cruel. At least I wasn't shunned by them, like a lot of the other girls who didn't have brains, looks, or a quick wit to make the in-crowd notice them.

While I downplayed my intelligence, at the same time, I used it to tutor the dumb athletes and the dumb Important Others. Giving me some credibility and usefulness to the Popular Ones. Although they were using me, I didn't mind, for I was getting what I wanted. Acceptance, Recognition, and Popularity.

In high school, my best friend was a girl named Barbara who lived in a project on the next block. Barbara was exceptionally smart and somewhat of an introvert. An elitist introvert. Although she participated in some extracurricular activities, she was more attracted to the intellectual side of life. Barbara came from a large family of twelve kids, with a mother and a father. She, too, had problems communicating with her mother. But unlike me, Barbara wasn't the oldest. She was next to the youngest. And she often ignored her mother's scolding. Her mother didn't whip her like Mama whipped her children. In fact, Barbara's mother didn't whip her at all.

I liked going over to Barbara's house. Even though they had a lotta, lotta roaches. We often did our homework assignments together at the dining room table, with the roaches crawling all around the table, floor and walls. Because we were both in the honors division, we had many of the same classes. We often philosophied about our lives and futures. Barbara didn't have the same hang-up that I had about being accepted by the in-crowd. She viewed them as a bunch of silly, foolish kids. So she tended to downplay their popularity and importance. But I was determined that I would be accepted as part of the in-crowd.

At some point during my high school years, I began to think that I was totally accepted by the in-crowd. After all, I was a member of the GAA (Girls Athletic Association), Future Teachers of America, Future Business Leaders of America, concert band and concert orchestra, and drama club. I even had my picture in one of the city's leading newspapers that was taken when the concert band was participating in a citywide competition. During my senior year I ran for president of the Student Senate and lost by only a slim margin.

I helped found and became the editor of the student newspaper. I was on top of the world when *The Chicago Tribune* printed an article I had written. The article was about one of my nosy neighbors. I proudly showed that article to all of my neighbors and church friends. One neighbor, Mrs. Johnson, recognized the "nosy neighbor" as being herself. She asked me if the article was about her.

I replied, "No, Mrs. Johnson, I just made that up."

But the article was really about Mrs. Johnson, one of the nosiest persons that ever walked the face of the earth. Forever peeping from behind her curtains, looking at everything that went on the porch, the comings and goings, knowing everybody's business. Yes, the article was about her, but I vehemently denied it.

As editor of the school newspaper, I was privy to the press meetings with the stars. I even met Marlon Brando and Alfred Hitchcock and got their autographs.

I also developed a column for the lovelorn, entitled *Ask Lorraine*. I made up a love problem situation, drawing upon my own life experience, for that first column, in which I wrote about a love-smitten girl who had a crush on a particular boy. I wrote about me and Arthur, although I changed his name and gave myself a pseudonym. I really did still have a slight crush on him, even though we never dated again after that freshman dance. But I was still trying to get his attention. So I wrote about some encounters we had had and how he had rebuffed my efforts. I ended the letter asking "Lorraine" what should I do to get him to notice me.

When that issue came out, Arthur angrily approached me because he knew that I was the editor of the student newspaper. "Mai, is that letter about me?"

Oh, no, I thought, *he's really pissed off.* So I lied. "No, Arthur, someone sent in that letter. I don't know who wrote it." *Well, it just better not be about me, now or never!* With that conversation, I ended my *Ask Lorraine* foray. Besides, none of the other students sent in not even one letter asking for romantic advice. So that was the end of *Ask Lorraine. Lesson learnt—sometimes it's necessary to tell a lie to maintain good relations.*

***

I loved the basketball team and would often cheer them on in their games. The school cheer, *"We're from Lane Tech, Mighty Mighty Lane Tech. Everywhere we go, people wannna know who we are. So we tell them. We're from Lane Tech, Mighty Mighty Lane Tech.* The school song, *Lane, we're here for you. We wear your colors red and blue. Red for courage bright, blue for loyal hearts, and ever faithful is our cry. Wherever we go, we'll let them know that we are here from Lane Tech High.* The high school basketball games were fun and exciting, especially when my team won. The school spirit and adrenalin were so high you could feel it reverberating throughout the school. Oh, but when the other team won—that was another story. My high school friends would be waiting at the bus that transported the other team to cause them bodily harm. Often someone would find a couple of

2X4s and try to ram the bus with them. No, my school did not like losing.

***

My mother had the annoying habit of showing up at my school to make sure that I was attending class. I would look out at the window of the classroom door and see her standing by the door, peering into the classroom. Sometimes, one of my friends would tell me that my mother had been at school talking to my teachers. I was horrified. No other parent checked up on their children like that. At least once a month, especially during the first two years Mama was at the school checking up on me. I was teased by my classmates. *"Why yo' Mama checking up on you?"* It was an extremely unpleasant situation for me. Not only was my mother embarrassing me by her presence at the school, but I bore the brunt of my classmates' jokes about it.

I did have several memorable experiences with my teachers at the high school. During my freshman year I took a chemistry class. I did the bare minimum of work but managed to get a "C" overall average. However, when midterm report card came, Mrs. Foster, the chemistry teacher, gave me a "D." (A "D" was a low grade, right before an "F," which meant you failed the class.) I had never received a grade that low before and was sure that Mama would be pissed off, maybe to the point of whipping me.

I approached Mrs. Foster about the grade. "Mrs. Foster, why did you give me a D? My grades averaged a C."

"Yes, I know. But you could do much better. You didn't really try to live up to your potential. Other students struggled to get a C, and I gave it to them. But you, you really didn't put any effort into your assignments and tests. So this D is a challenge for you to do better."

After that conversation with Mrs. Foster I became serious about my chemistry studies and redoubled my efforts to do better. My final grade was a "B," next to the highest grade of "A."

Another experience involved an incident with my drama teacher, Mr. Ford. The drama class would spend time rehearsing after school, working hard to present a play to the school. Those rehearsals usually lasted about an hour. However, one afternoon the rehearsal lasted two hours. When I returned home, Mama was up in arms and about to whip me for being so late in coming home.

"What took you so long to get home? I'm going to whip you!"

"Why, Mama? I was at school rehearsing for the play."

"No you weren't! No rehearsal lasts that long. You were messing with some boy!"

"No, Mama, please don't whip me. You can call the teacher. He'll tell you that I was rehearsing for the play!"

So that time, Mama gave me the benefit of the doubt. Early the next morning, however, she called the school to speak with Mr. Ford who verified that I, indeed, was at rehearsal. At rehearsal that day, Mr. Ford told the class that the rehearsal would stay within the allotted time limit because he didn't want any more mothers calling him, sneeringly looking directly at me.

Gym classes were a farce, whether you were on your period or not. I took swimming one semester and nearly drowned. I was in the deep end of the pool and panicked. I went under and kept screaming for help and flailing my arms. The gym teacher, knowing that I was a class clown, looked at me and continued to work with the other students. I felt myself drowning. I couldn't breathe. All I could do was holler the couple of times that I was able to raise my head above the water. Finally, noticing that I was in real distress, the gym teacher jumped into the swimming pool and pulled me to safety. After that harrowing experience, I never tried to learn to swim again, at least not in deep water.

Another memorable gym experience was one with a teacher who was rumored to be an alcoholic. We could smell alcohol on her breath whenever she would let us get close to her. She would tell us "I don't care if you learn or not! I have my degree. You know my name. My initials are GP. You know what that stands for? Good Pussy!"

What a thing to say to some teenage girls! It showed no respect for us and certainly no respect for herself.

One other incident involved my physics teacher, Mr. Hall. One day in physics class, one of my classmates and I were having a conversation while Mr. Hall was talking. Mr. Hall saw only me talking and singled me out. I tried to protest, saying that I wasn't the only one talking out of turn in class. However, he would have none of it and insisted that I bring my mother to school for a disciplinary session. When my mother arrived at the school during the scheduled time for the session, she and I took our seats in the classroom, and Mr. Hall began talking about my behavior in class. How disruptive I was. How children should respect their elders. How I showed no respect for him by talking while he was talking. And my mother was agreeing with him, nodding her head in robust agreement. I just knew that I was going to get a severe whipping when we returned home. But then, Mr. Hall made a serious mistake. He said, "I don't care if it's Jesus Christ himself! Nobody talks out of turn in my class."

"Uh-oh," I thought, smiling inwardly, *"he done done it now!"*

Upon the mention of Jesus' name like that, my mother immediately stiffened. Her whole body language changed to that of ominous hostility. And her facial expression changed to one of horror, for Mr. Hall had taken the Lord's name in vain, one of Mama's major taboos. To take Jesus' name in vain was an outrage and, in her mind, proved that, not only wasn't he a Christian, but even worse, he was an out-and-out staunch heathen. And then he had the nerve to place himself above Jesus Christ! Privately, I smiled all the more, for I knew that I would not be getting a whipping that day because Mr. Hall's transgression was greater than mine. And sure enough, Mama did not whip me when we returned home.

***

I'll never forget the moment that I learned that President Kennedy had been assassinated. I was in physics class. Our teacher, Mr. Thymes, had just begun teaching our lesson for the day when he was called out of the classroom. Within a few minutes he returned to the classroom. Visibly unnerved and voice trembling, he announced that he had just been informed that President Kennedy had been assassinated. Upon hearing this news, the entire class became deadly silent, stunned, and in shock and disbelief. Although he tried to control himself, tears were streaming down Mr. Thymes' face, and most of the students were in tears, with some crying out loud. I sat frozen in my seat unable to move even one muscle.

"Oh, no. It can't be," several of us cried out.

"I'm afraid so," Mr. Thymes replied. Thoughts of President Kennedy rushed through my mind. How he was an advocate for civil rights and an advocate for peace and justice. How he had opened doors for so many Black folks. I thought of his beautiful wife and children and about what a loss his death was for the country. Unsurprisingly, there was no substantive physics lesson given that day. After giving the class a few moments for the news of President Kennedy's death to sink in, Mr. Thymes proceeded to teach the class as best as he could. But he taught in a robotic tone, as though he really wasn't there. He was just mouthing the words from the textbook. And none of us could pay attention anyway.

The rest of the day was just a blur.

***

As I grew older, my mother really began working my nerves, especially after I started working. The day I turned sixteen in my senior year of high school, I applied for and received my social security card.

Within a week I was hired as a waitress for the local community drug store, about six blocks from my house. (At that time, all of the community drug stores had a restaurant.) I worked after school at the restaurant and on Saturdays, making $1.00 an hour. So I was able to take home about $25.00 a week, which would come in really handy because I was entering my senior year and had to pay for my prom dress, class ring, and senior luncheon. So I told my mother that I was going to open up a savings account to save up money for the prom and other things. My mother told me that I didn't have to open up a savings account and that she would save my money for me. I saw nothing wrong with this and began giving her $5.00 each week to put aside for my graduation expenses.

I also had to give her almost half of my paycheck. I was only making a dollar an hour and Mama wanted half of that, saying that I had to pay my share of the household expenses. *What if I wasn't working? What about the household expenses then,* I angrily wondered. I could never save up to buy myself something nice. My mother was there every payday, just like a loan shark.

"Give me my money!"

"Your money! I worked my ass off for this!"

After so much bickering about money, I made a firm resolution to leave home by the time I turned eighteen, the legal age to leave home. Come hell or high water, I was getting the hell away from there.

In addition to the money I was beginning to earn, my job had another unexpected benefit. My mother didn't require me to watch my siblings. That responsibility fell to my younger sister, Berniece. So, whenever I got the chance, I gladly worked extra hours.

I really liked working at the restaurant. All of the staff were older than me and treated me like a little sister. My boss's name was Mr. Greene. Mr. Franklin was the general manager. One of my favorite waitresses was Rosemary. The dishwasher/cook was named Melvin, who was quite mature and handsome.

Because I had so much energy, I became quite efficient at waiting on customers, taking their orders, and even remembering their names. I would greet each customer with a smile, whether or not they returned one. Then I would courteously take their orders, patiently explaining items on the menus, and repeating their orders to make sure I had it right. Sometimes, some of the customers left tips. Most of the times, they didn't. I considered myself lucky to get a twenty-five cents tip. Some weeks I earned up to two dollars in tips.

I not only learned how to waitress but learned how to cook the food and operate the dishwasher and cash register as well. Once, when I was working in the kitchen of the restaurant, I dropped a steak on the floor while I was preparing to cook it. I was about to throw it in the garbage when Mr. Greene, out of the corner of his eye, saw me going to the garbage can with the steak in my hand. Mr.

Greene immediately stopped me, and in a loud voice, but not loud enough for the customers to hear it, said "Mai, What are you doing?"

"I'm throwing the steak away because I dropped it on the floor," I replied.

"Oh no, we don't throw away any food here. Rinse it off and put it on the grill and serve it," he commanded.

Although I felt bad about serving a customer a steak that had fallen on the floor, I followed Mr. Greene's orders. And the customer couldn't tell the difference.

Another time, I was in the locker room with Rosemary, putting on my waitress uniform to prepare to go to work. Rosemary was smoking a cigarette as she so often did. She seemed so cool doing so, so sophisticated. I had seen cigarettes advertised on television, but I didn't know too much about them because nobody I knew smoked them. Rosemary asked if I wanted a cigarette. Trying to be grown, I replied that I did. Rosemary took a cigarette from her pack of unfiltered Pall Malls and gave one to me.

"I think I'll save it until after I get off work," I told her. So I put the cigarette on the shelf in my locker and went to work. That cigarette stayed there for about a week until I could summon up enough nerve to smoke it. So, one evening after work, I took a book of matches from the counter of the restaurant and put it in my uniform pocket. I decided to smoke the cigarette when no one else was in the locker room. Gingerly, I perched the cigarette between my lips, like I saw Rosemary do so many times. With the cigarette firmly anchored between my lips, I struck a match and lit it. When I inhaled it, like I saw Rosemary doing, I straight away gagged and choked. My eyes watered. My body seemingly went into convulsions. I gagged some more. I choked some more. Then I gagged and choked some more. After I regained my composure and knew that I would not choke to death, I put that cigarette out and resolved to never touch one again. Poor me, I didn't know that cigarettes get stronger if left in the open air, especially after a week of lying on a locker shelf.

***

Sometimes, my mother would come to the restaurant to watch me at work. She would order a piece of cake or pie because she didn't have enough money to order a meal. She never said anything to me about my work; she just watched what I was doing.

I was such a good worker that Mr. Greene often praised me. Within six months, Mr. Franklin offered me a job in the drug store itself, operating the cash register. Plus, I got a raise to $1.25 an hour! I was elated. In my new position, I started out with a "bank" of $25 in cash and change. At the end of my shift, the cash register receipts had to match the money in my drawer plus the $25 bank. And I was very accurate in counting money and giving customers the correct change. I was even more so meticulous about that because cashiers had to make up the difference if their cash register was short.

***

The store had its share of shoplifters. Shoplifters caused the store to lose money, and they were dealt with severely. So part of my job was to be on the lookout for shoplifters. I remembered one case when Mr. Greene and Mr. Franklin took a man, who had been shoplifting, to the back office. I, as well as the customers who were in the store, could hear the vicious and sadistic punches administered by Mr. Greene and Mr. Franklin. We could hear the man groaning, screaming, and crying out in pain, begging them to stop.

"Are you going to shoplift again?", they asked him.

"No, no, I swear I won't."

They continued to beat him until they were sure that he had learned his lesson, and needless to say, he didn't shoplift again. At least not at my store.

Another time, I was sure that a little old white woman was shoplifting. That woman would often come into the store. She looked like poor white trash and had an unpleasant smell about her. She would purchase one or two small items and leave. But one time, she hung around the store for an awfully long time, and I was sure that I saw that woman put something into her purse. So I told Mr. Franklin that I thought that the woman was shoplifting. Mr. Franklin pulled the woman to the side of the store and made her open up her purse. After looking through her purse, he didn't find anything that was shoplifted. I felt really bad about that; that I had wrongly accused someone. That little old woman did not come back into the store after that.

Within another four months, I had excelled in my job so well as a cashier that the pharmacist, Mr. Hunter, asked me to be his assistant. Mr. Hunter was a kindly man, tall, handsome, light-skinned a little on the heavy side, with gray eyes, and curly hair. I was thrilled at the opportunity to work in the pharmacy and fill prescriptions. He taught me how to read prescriptions and how to look on the shelves for the correct medicines. I would proudly stand behind the pharmacy counter, take the customers' prescriptions, and fill some of them. Of course, Mr. Hunter always checked behind me. In the few months that I worked in that position, I made only one mistake, which, of course, Mr. Hunter caught. *Lesson learnt—be diligent. Hard work pays off.*

***

Also in my senior year (after I finally turned the magical age of sixteen), my mother allowed me to begin dating.

My first real date, without my mother chaperoning me, was with Melvin, my fellow coworker at the restaurant. Melvin was several years older than me. Before he asked me out, he asked my age. I told him that I was eighteen. So Melvin took me to an elegant downtown restaurant, an Italian restaurant, with an indoor garden, a flowing stream of water which wrangled its way through a well-defined path in the restaurant, and a proliferation of multicolored flowers, ferns, and trees. As we were talking, I inadvertently told Melvin that I was seventeen. His eyes bucked wide open in shock.

"You told me that you were eighteen!", he said.

"Well, I said that because I'm almost eighteen. I'll be eighteen in a few months."

For some reason that I didn't understand, Melvin didn't ask me out again. Poor me, I didn't know the meaning of jail bait and that Melvin wasn't going to risk that I would not be turning eighteen.

Shortly after the date with Melvin, I began dating Larry, whom I had met at church. Well, not really dating, because Larry didn't have any money to take me anywhere. So I guess you could call it "courting". Larry attended church every Sunday. Because I had met him in church and because he and his family were regular church-goers, my mother immediately approved of him. I liked him a lot, sometimes even thinking that I was in love with him. I would see him at church on Sundays, and many times during the week he would take the bus to my job just to walk me home after work. Oftentimes, his brother, Jeremiah, would accompany us on those walks home. We had so much fun talking, laughing, and joking during the six-block walk.

Mama even let Larry come to the house to visit. We would sit around with my sisters and brothers and play board games, watch TV, and just talk. Mama really liked him because he was so well-man-nered and would say "yes ma'am" and "no ma'am" to her. When no one was around, which was a real rarity, he and I would often sneak a kiss. Real, tongue-touching, French-mouthing kisses. He was so tender. And he would hold me like I was so fragile. It was hard find-ing those moments because my brothers and sisters would always be peeping around the living room corner to see if they could catch us kissing, and Mama would periodically walk through to make sure that we were keeping a respectable distance from each other. If she thought we were sitting too close, she would loudly clear her throat. "Ahem!" And Larry and I would immediately move away from each other on the couch or stop holding hands.

Sometimes, when he walked me home from my job, we would walk up the stairs to my apartment because the elevators were bro-ken. All seven flights. But it was a real treat, when no one had pissed or shitted in the stairwell. For on those flights up, we would stop at each landing and kiss and hug. Sometimes he would even gently feel my little breasts (28A) or tenderly rub the front of my pussy. Sometimes, those moves would frighten me because I knew by now, thanks to my fast girlfriends, that those were the first moves of a boy trying to "do it" to a girl. But it excited me so! I would get all woozy and weak-kneed. My little heart would start beating so fast that I could hardly contain myself. And sometimes, little wet fluid would ooze out from my thing.

I really liked Larry. But I would never "do it" with him or anyone else because I was so scared of getting pregnant. Even though I was in my senior year, I still wasn't sure what it took to get pregnant. All I knew was that if you "did it," you would get pregnant. I didn't know what all "doing it" entailed. I just knew that it probably had something to do with a boy putting his thing in you. And if I got pregnant, Mama would get mad, and I didn't want to make Mama mad, at least not about that. I was more scared of Mama than of God. After all, I didn't know what type of punishment God would inflict if I had gotten pregnant (the burning fires of hell were so distant!). But I knew the types of painful whippings my mother could administer. And if Mama would beat the living hell out of me for being smart-mouthed, I could only imagine the horrendous type of beating I would get if I got pregnant. Mama would beat me worse than she had beat Robert, if that was possible. So I never let Larry or anyone else get into my panties.

Larry thought I was pretty! Imagine that! Someone thought that I was pretty! I had long since given up on sleeping with clothespins on my nose and lips and stopped using the Nadinola. None of those had helped change my looks for the better anyway. So I had accepted myself as being an ugly duckling. After all, that was what the in-crowd had implicitly implied. I was not light-skinned. I didn't have "good" hair and a thin nose and had absolutely no breasts to mention. So I was utterly thrilled that Larry was not only paying me some attention but also thought that I was pretty. Larry was the first guy I had dated since my freshman date with Arthur. (The date with Melvin didn't count.) Not that I had boys on my mind or anything like that. But it sure was nice to have someone to pay attention to me and someone I could call my boyfriend.

Larry was real popular among the girls at church. In fact, he was dating several of us at the same time. Of course, he would always deny it and tell each one of us that she was the only one. Years later, he confessed that the only reason he joined that church was because of all the girls who attended.

I got to be real good friends with Larry's sisters, especially the two that were closest to me in age, Yolanda and Susanne. Yolanda and I were tightest of tights. Mama even let me spend some nights at Larry's house. Mama gave me permission to do so only because Larry and his family (including his mother) attended the same church. What Mama didn't know! I had so much fun at Larry's house. He came from a large family (thirteen), and all of them lived together, and Larry had a father, a real father, living at home! He was a quiet soft-spoken man and never had too much to say to me, unlike Larry's mother who was quite outspoken and really liked me and treated me just like one of her own children. I would help fix breakfast and dinner. And we would have parties, dance, and play cards! Card playing was forbidden in my house because, according to Mama, playing cards was the devil's game. It didn't matter what kind of card game it was. In fact, we couldn't even play Monopoly because you had to roll the dice to play the game, and, according to Mama, dice were a tool of the devil.

During my senior year, I also began dating William. Imagine! Two boyfriends! William was on the varsity basketball team. A second string player but on the varsity team nevertheless. And he was certainly no catch. He was so ugly that the other students called him the "Monster." He was jet black (which was not acceptable), big, and gangly. He had a huge head, a big pug nose, and thick massive lips. But, because he was a basketball player, one of The Athletes, he was accepted into the in-crowd. And his acceptance guaranteed my acceptance. Besides, he was the best friend of Chris, one of the most popular and most prestigious and best dressers and most s-m-o-o-t-h-e-s-t guys in school. All of the girls ooohed and aaahed over him. Even me. Even though he was my old man's best friend. He was handsome. He was suave. He was smart. And he lived on the South side—a true mark of distinction to the West side crowd.

One day, during our senior year, the three of us (William, Chris, and I) decided to throw a party at Chris' house. Mama agreed to the party because Edna agreed to chaperone it. Chris put me in charge of making all of the arrangements for the party. I eagerly began planning the menu, the music, the date, and the time and sent out invitations. As a courtesy to Chris, I mailed him an invitation to the party. I was so proud! Me! A peripheral in-crowder throwing a party with the Ultimate in-crowder! I was the *bomb*! I had finally arrived! Chris approached me in school the day after he received his invitation in the mail and was quite distraught.

"Oh, Mai, did you make out all of the invitations like this?", he asked, for I had written on the invitation that *I* was giving the party at Chris's house.

"Yeah, I did," I replied. *"What's wrong with it?"*

"Oh, no! Mai. You should have written that I was giving the party. The party's ruined. Now, no one is going to come. Mai, there's a difference between popularity and prestige!"

And, as it turned out, the party was not well attended. I reasoned that the poor turnout could have been due to the fact that it was held on the South side and most people lived on the West side, and it was wintertime and it was cold. But Chris was sure otherwise. And in my heart of hearts, I agreed with him. For the in-crowd didn't turn out to party with me. I realized that there is indeed a difference between popularity and prestige. Although I was popular, I didn't have the necessary prestige to impress the in-crowd. That party ended my foray into the inner circle of the in-crowd for I learned that, no matter how much I cow-towed to them, I would never be accepted by them. *Lesson learnt—prestige is better than popularity. One day I would have prestige.*

***

Another major disaster for me that occurred during my senior year was the prom, which was held in June. William and I had broken up about three months or so before the prom. No biggie for me for I had met a senior named Wendell in March of that year, while riding the bus, who lived on the South side and was interested in me. He often called me, came to visit me several times, and even had taken me to the movies several times. He went to one of those fancy private Catholic schools on the South side. That was a feather in my cap, to be dating a guy from the South side. He even had his own car!

And smoked cigarettes! Yep, I have truly arrived. He had invited me to his prom, and I invited him to my prom. I didn't ask Larry to take me to the prom because he was too poor and never had any money. He couldn't afford to take me to the movies, let alone to the prom. Even though he was my official boyfriend, he understood my going to the prom with Wendell. He told me to have a good time. Poor thing, he couldn't even afford to go to his own prom. But he acted like it was no big deal.

Because I had no checking or savings account (didn't really know anything about them), my mother had been saving my money for me. Remember, she told me that there was no reason to open up a savings account and that she would save my money for me. I was earning about $25 a week, which seemed like a lot of money. Every payday, from October through April, I had been giving her at least $5 to "put away" to pay for my senior prom, prom dress, class ring, year book, and senior luncheon. This was in addition to the "household" contribution that I had to make to her. Even though I was initially leery about this arrangement, my mother convinced me that it was a good one, that my money was safely tucked away in her secret hiding place in the house. I figured that, by June, I would have almost $200, which was more than enough. The ring was $35–$75; the luncheon was $25; senior prom was $30; the yearbook was $20; and after-prom dinner was $25, leaving me about $60 to buy the best prom dresses money could buy.

In the months leading up to the prom, I was so excited. Some of my classmates and I constantly talked about the prom. Extravagant plans were made. Barbara had decided that she was not going to the prom but went shopping with me to help pick out my dresses. *How wise I have been*, I exclaimed to myself. *I've been saving up for almost seven months. I don't have to get a cheap prom dress. I am going to look good! Only the best for me!*

So Barbara and I made almost weekly excursions to the Black trendy shopping districts, on 63rd and Halsted and on Pulaski and Madison, even venturing downtown, looking at and pricing prom dresses, trying them on. I knew that I would need two dresses: one for my prom and one for Wendell's prom.

Finally, I decided upon the two dresses that I would buy. I approached Mama toward the end of April and asked for the money to buy the dresses.

"*Money? What money?*"

"*The money that I've been giving to you to put aside for me.*"

"*Oh, child, I don't have that money.*"

"*What did you do with it? It was mine! You were supposed to be saving it for me.*"

"*Oh, I used it to pay for household expenses. It cost more than what you were giving me to feed you and pay these bills!*"

I went to my room and broke down and cried. No, I bawled. Words could not explain the searing emotional pain I felt surging throughout my body. I was devastated! In tears. Heartbroken. Distraught. Betrayed. Deceived. For almost eight months Mama had told me that she was saving my money for me. Yet, she had spent all of my hard-earned money and wasn't even remorseful about it, and, although the prom was still two months away, she made no attempt to replace it. And she acted like she had an attitude because I had asked her for my money!

Because of the meager amount of money that I was earning and the shortness of time before the proms (two months), it was impossible for me to save enough money to buy the two dresses or even one nice dress. And so, I ended up wearing the same dress to both proms. A dress so cheap, I was truly embarrassed to wear it. A dress that loudly and powerfully proclaimed the words *"Cheap! Cheap!"* Poor me. I could only save $20 for my dress because I had to pay for my class ring, senior prom, and after-prom dinner. My dress wound up costing $19.99. An ugly, floor-length pale blue dress with semi-spaghetti straps, layered with cheap white lace. And I couldn't even afford to get my hair done for the prom.

Wendell was embarrassed, too. For he had wanted his prom lady to have style, to show her off in front of his South side friends, and I didn't have it. No style at all. His look plainly showed his embarrassment when he picked me up in his fine car. And he was looking so good in his black tuxedo. He took me to his prom, but he couldn't show me off. I looked like a project girl, a charity case.

He barely introduced me to his friends and, for the most part, kept me away from them. He took me home directly after the prom. We didn't even go to the after-prom dinner or party. He didn't even kiss me good night. But he was honorable, true to his word. He told me that he would see me the following week for my prom. I was home before 11:30 p.m.

For my prom, Mama had told me to be home by midnight.

"Midnight!," I screamed. *"The prom isn't over until midnight."*

"Well, you don't have to stay until it's over."

I felt so ashamed to have to wear the same cheap dress to my prom. Here I was, trying to be somebody. And my mother had totally screwed me up. I didn't even try to explain to Wendell why my dress was so cheap and why I was wearing the same dress to both proms, and Wendell didn't say anything about it. But, then again, he hardly said anything at all and was quite distant from me. After my prom, at which both of us had a miserable time, we attended the after-prom dinner at a swanky hotel because I had already paid for both of our meals. During the prom and dinner, I tried to show off my South side date to my West side friends, but he wasn't too cooperative, didn't try to make small talk, and wasn't too friendly at all. He barely danced with me all night. After the dinner, he took me straight home. Didn't even kiss me good night. It was after 3:00 a.m. when I returned home. I thought that Mama was going to kill me. She was up, waiting for me. But to my surprise, Mama didn't say a word. She just looked at me when I opened the door and stepped inside.

As for Wendell, I never heard from him again. After that, he probably never again dated another girl from the West side.

I also had to get the cheapest class ring ($35) and could not attend the senior luncheon. This incident seriously damaged the level of trust I had in my mother. I could accept the beatings, but I could not accept the fact that I had entrusted my hard-earned money to my mother who had spent it all and did not tell me. If she had told me what she was doing, I could have asked to work some extra hours at the restaurant to make it up. But she didn't tell me and made no attempt to replace it, and did not attempt to borrow it, which she could have easily done from her brother, Harry, and felt no remorse about it. That was a bitter pill for me to swallow and deepened the rift between me and Mama. I harbored a deep resentment toward Mama for that act of deception, and it took over fifty years for me to forgive her for that. And even though I eventually forgave her, I never forgot it. *Lesson learnt—don't trust anyone to save your money for you, especially if they hardly have any money themselves.*

***

I would sometimes have to encourage myself to live with my situation. One of my favorite songs was *You'll Never Walk Alone*. I knew that my time living with my mother would end when I turned eighteen years old, come hell or high water. So I would encourage myself to walk on through the wind and storms, with hope in my heart.

I had never entertained the thought of running away from home like my brother Robert had done. For he had to return back home, having nowhere else to go. That was a memorable occasion—Robert's foray into running away. When he was thirteen, Robert announced to us one afternoon that he was running away from home.

"Oh?", Mama said.

Berniece and I were ecstatic! No longer would we have to defend ourselves against him. No longer would he be able to steal our hard-earned money from us. No longer would he be around to tell lies on us.

"Yes," Robert said, "I'm running away today."

Mama replied that he could, indeed, run away, but he could only take what he had bought. Robert was crushed because he had packed a few clothes in his bag.

"Where are you going with that?", Mama asked. "I told you that you could only take what you bought! And I bought those clothes!"

Robert looked exasperated. "Well, at least can I take a can of soup with me?"

"Yes, you can take a can of soup, but not a can opener."

So, with that, Robert defiantly walked out the door. Berniece and I were surprised that Mama didn't make him go out butt naked because she had bought the clothes he was wearing. Around ten that night we heard a timid knock on the door. It was Robert! Returning home, defeated, because he had nowhere to go.

So I knew that I would not be running away because I, too, had nowhere to go. And I also knew that once I left, I would not be returning. I knew that life had something better to offer, only I didn't know what it was. But I kept the thought of leaving Mama firmly planted in my heart, not knowing how it would come to fruition. *Lesson learnt—keep on believing. Somehow things will work out for the better.*

***

Throughout high school, I maintained a high grade point average and was on the Honor Roll most of the time, as well as the National Honor Society. During my senior year, I began to think about attending college. I had never really thought about college because very few of my classmates, and even fewer of the in-crowd, valued a college education.

I approached my high school counselor to formulate some college plans. Although I was in the top ten percent of my class and had been consistently on the Honor Roll and was a member of the National Honor Society, Mrs. Vann counseled me to enroll in a community junior college to acquire an AA degree. After that, I could become a secretary. Then I could attend Chicago Teachers College South (the college for Black students wanting to become teachers, Chicago Teachers College North was for the white kids) and become a teacher. I thought that was good advice, become a secretary and then a teacher. Other than being a blue-collar worker, there were very few career options that Black people could pursue. Back then, the only viable jobs for Blacks, other than working in factories or other menial jobs, were to become postmen or school teachers.

One day, while chatting with Barbara between classes, she informed me that there were college recruiters from downstate Knave College at the school.

"College recruiters? Really? What do they do? And why are they here?"

After Barbara explained that they were looking for students to attend their college, she suggested that I go to the auditorium to talk with them. Go away to school? I had never thought about that! It was the perfect solution to my problems at home. A way I could leave my mother and still be held in high esteem at the same time. I wasn't sure that I would be accepted at that college, but I thought it was worth a try. So I went to the auditorium to speak to the recruiters and was utterly astounded that they were interested in me because Mrs. Vann had told me that the best I could do was go to a community junior college and become a secretary. I didn't know any better. I didn't know anyone who had been to college other than my uncle and his wife. And they had never said a word to me about attending college. I had no idea that I could aspire to something better than a junior college. I took the application home that they handed me, filled it out, and mailed it to the college. Mrs. Vann wasn't particularly encouraging. She just faked a passing interest. Probably so I wouldn't be so devastated when I was denied admission.

After a couple of weeks, I, along with a group of about three other students from my school, received an invitation to spend a weekend at the college campus! The trip was free, and the recruiters made all of the arrangements. I eagerly went along with school friends, Barbara, Yolanda, and Edward. Students from other high schools were also there.

Upon arrival that Friday evening, I was awed by the campus' expansive beauty. I had never, ever seen that much green grass before, except at the parks. And the parks' grass wasn't nearly as pretty and well-manicured as the college's. The campus had modern buildings that were strategically distanced from one another, the science building, the PE building, the library, the student union building, and the student dorms. I had never seen anything like it. All of my prior learning had taken place in one building.

There was so much space! Living in the city and in the projects, I had become accustomed to crowded buildings, places, and spaces. It was a life-changing experience for me.

I got to stay in a dorm, something I had only read about. I was ecstatic! For the first time in many years, I shared a bedroom with only one other person, my college roommate for the weekend. Ever since my sister April was born, I had to share a bedroom with my two sisters. I thought I was in heaven. A whole weekend of not having to watch my sisters and brothers and not having to listen to my mother. It was great!

I mingled with the college students and other high school students that the college had recruited and went on a tour of the campus. The college professors even took time to speak with the visiting group.

The college cooks prepared scrumptious meals for us. That Friday evening, we had a bar-be-que on the patio, accompanied by a live band performance. For dinner that Saturday evening, we had T-bone steaks, charbroiled to perfection on the outdoor grills! I had never eaten steak before in my whole life. It was delicious and served sizzling hot. And so juicy and tender! Melt-in-your-mouth tender. Served with garlic bread, salad, and baked potatoes and soft drinks.

There was one thing, though. Most of the students were white. I had never been around that many white people before. With the exception of a summer Shakespeare Theater program during my junior year, the only white people I knew were a couple of school teachers, those women case workers who came around periodically asking probing questions that were none of their business, and a couple of white folks my mother worked for. The visiting high school group met a couple of Black students who told us that they really liked the college. Little did I know then that there were literally only a couple of Black students at that college.

What was more amazing was that these white people wanted me to attend their college. They told me that I was smart and would have no problems academically. They told me that Knave was one of the best private colleges in the nation. I was proud that they even bothered with me, a poor Black girl from the ghetto, the projects no less. I hoped and fervently prayed that they would accept me.

About a month after my visit, I received a letter of acceptance from Knave. I quickly completed and returned the acceptance letter and began the process of completing the financial aid forms. The financial aid application was quite intrusive, asking questions about our family income, composition, and housing arrangements. It was during this process that those white women—those case workers, who always asked my mother questions that were none of their business—began to ask me questions. They asked me questions about attending college, how I felt about it, and that they were proud of me, like they knew me. I was quite insulted by it all. Even more insulting, downright humiliating, was the fact that I had to inform Knave College that I was on welfare because the college had to send an income verification form to the welfare people for me to qualify for financial aid. Now, everybody at that school would know that I was poor. But I swallowed my pride, completed and mailed in the forms, and subsequently received a full scholarship package, having to take out only a small loan and agree to be a work-study student.

My high school graduation was a blast! I proudly walked across the stage as my name was called, amid loud cheers from my family. After the graduation ceremony, Larry took me to dinner at Ronnie's Steak House in downtown Chicago, which was *the* place to go. It was the second time in my life that I had steak. It was then that Larry told me that he was not going to go to college but that he was joining the Navy instead.

So, over the summer, we made our plans. He would spend four years in the Navy, while I spent the four years in college. Then we would get married.

Oh yeah. I finally learned how girls became pregnant. My older sister told me. Edna told me that, until the birth of her first baby, she thought that she had become pregnant by kissing her boyfriend, Fred. After all, Mama kept telling her (as well as me) that you get pregnant by kissing "dem boys." After Edna's baby was born, she told the nurse, "Whew! I'll never do that again!"

"Do what, baby?"

"Kiss another boy."

"Baby, that's not how you got pregnant!"

And so, Edna learned that she became pregnant through engaging in unprotected sexual intercourse. Mama never mentioned sexual intercourse. And that's what happens when you don't keep your legs closed like Mama had admonished.

***

One of the saddest things that happened during my high school years was the death of my grandmother. My grandmother died while I was a sophomore in high school. When I learned of my grandmother's death, I truly grieved. My grief was made worse because my mother could not afford to take me Down South for the funeral. Even though my grandmother's death grievously saddened me, I always felt, throughout my life, that my grandmother was watching over me, protecting me. I would sometimes talk to my grandmother, visualize her presence, and would always see her sweet, sweet smile. I never lost that connection with her. *Lesson learnt—just because someone's dead doesn't mean that they're gone.*

And so, those chapters of my life were over. My growing up years. The elementary and junior high school years. My high school years. I was going away. Away to newfound adventures, a college life and a life without Mama. A life where I was free to do what I wanted to do and go where I wanted to go, free of Mama's constant oversight and nagging. A life free of having to babysit my younger brothers and sisters. A life where I could explore life. Unfettered, picturing myself as a free spirit running unleashed and totally free to explore new environments.

I was going to a college that was predominantly white, exposing me to a race of people with whom I had never had close contact. Although I felt a little trepidation, it wasn't such a frightening prospect. But I knew nothing of the covert racism awaiting me on that beautiful college campus. However, my fears were assuaged by the knowledge that two other students from my high school would be attending the same college. And there were a few other Black students who would be attending, so I really wouldn't really be alone.

I didn't know what college would be like. After all, no one in my family had attended college except my uncle, and he never talked about college to me. All I knew was that living on campus could not be worse than living at home.

On the three-hour drive to the college, all I could think about was my newly found freedom. A life where I would meet new friends. What adventures awaited me! Sure, I would miss my friends, but there was so much more to life. I would sorely miss Larry, who was going to enlist in the Navy while I attended college. And after our four-year stints, we would get married, a thought that I thoroughly relished. But for now, all I could think about was that, by the grace of God, I was free to start a new life. *Lesson learnt—God will make a way somehow.*

***

So many thoughts permeated my mind on that journey to the college campus. As we drove down the highway with its endless corn fields, I reflected on the lessons learnt throughout my young life:

> *No matter how much you want it to be so, sometimes life just isn't fair.*
> *Trust your own memories.*
> *There truly is such a thing as unconditional love.*
> *Racism exists, whether you recognize it or not.*
> *Don't bite off more than you can chew.*
> *Life is a process of constant change. Make the best of it.*
> *Unconditional love has no time limits. It's always there.*
> *The Holy Spirit must be a powerful thing. It can make you do irrational, unexplainable things. Better not mess with it!*
>
> *Lesson relearnt—racism still exists.*
> *Racism is alive and well and you better not cross the lines.*
> *Negroes better "stay in their place" or suffer for breaking Jim Crow rules.*
> *You don't always need a doctor. The body can heal itself.*
> *Believe in yourself and follow through on that belief, no matter what others may think or say.*

All fathers aren't good men; some are just dirty old men.

Don't keep painful experiences to yourself. Others have been through what you're going through.

Don't blame others for circumstances over which they had no control.

When someone tells you that they're tired of you messing with them, you'd better believe it!

Money can get you out of some painful things.

Listen to the experts.

Life goes on, cherish the memories.

You can't change a person who does not want to change.

Sometimes it's beyond your ability to understand why some people stay in bad situations.

Curiosity is an inquisitive creature that can lead you to places that you would otherwise never explore.

Being black is undesirable.

Don't depend on anyone else; learn to do for yourself.

Just because you're born into it doesn't mean that you like your family, but there's nothing you can do about it. Make the best of it.

No matter if you do get your ass beat, don't let nobody walk all over you.

Sometimes bad things can work on your behalf.

A friend can be your worst enemy.

Try to live up to your own expectations and no one else's.

Sometimes it's necessary to tell a lie to maintain good relations.

Be diligent. Hard work pays off.

Prestige is better than popularity.

Don't trust anyone to save your money for you, especially if they hardly have any money themselves.

ABOUT THE AUTHOR

Alfreda Williams has a master's degree from the University of Chicago School of Social Service Administration and has worked extensively in the field of youth development. She has garnered numerous awards for her work in youth and community development and was listed as one of the Outstanding Women of America.

Keep on believing. Somehow things will work out for the better.
Just because someone's dead doesn't mean that they're gone.
God will make a way somehow.